Game On!

Boys! 2

Minecraft Madness

Written and Illustrated by Kate Cullen
Copyright © 2015 @ Kate Cullen
ISBN 978 1515046646

Dedication

To all the gamers out there who

haven't forgotten to keep reading as well.

If you don't like to laugh,

If you don't like a bit of action,

If you don't like smelly jokes,

This book won't be to your satisfaction,

If you don't like to poke fun at,

and annoy your big sister

If you can't stand computer games,

and you'd rather play Twister,

then you better not read this book!!!!

BUT

If you do like that stuff,

then this book is for you.

AND

Before you read it, you may like to get my **FREE** Ebook too,

Game on Boys 1: The PlayStation Playoffs.

At Amazon or other retailers

If you wish to be notified when other awesome titles by this author are released
please send a quick line to the below email
gameonboysseries@gmail.com

CONTENTS

1. Saved By Minecraft

Noooooooooo! I can not believe it. I can not  believe this is happening to me again. What is wrong with my family? Don't they have any intelligence or common sense, or any brains for that matter? How many times are they going to ruin my life? I'm sure there is some microchip in my mom's brain that sets off an alarm when everything is going along awesomely for me. "DING!" it goes. "Things are going well for Ryan. Time to set a bomb to detonate disaster for him," says Mom's Siri messenger in her brain.

Actually I'm not sure my mom has a brain sometimes. Maybe she does, but she definitely doesn't have a heart; not when it comes to me anyway. When it comes to me, my mom's heart is made of rock.

When it comes to my sister Lisa though, it's a different story. Where Lisa is concerned, my mom's heart is as big as an elephant's bum. What Lisa wants, Lisa gets. If Lisa wants a biscuit, she gets a whole

packet. If she wants a Dvd, Mom gets her five. If she wants a phone, she gets the latest and the best.

If Lisa does something wrong, Mom forgives her and says it was the cat's fault, even though we don't have a cat. But when I do something wrong, I get life imprisonment.

Life can be so unfair when there's a 'Lisa' involved. I suppose I have to suck it up and feel sorry for her, because Mom gives her all these things to make up for the fact that she has a smaller IQ than a toothbrush. In case you don't know, an IQ is your intelligence level, and Lisa's is right down there next to ants and worms.

Ok, I know I'm sounding really spiteful, like I have middle child, psycho syndrome, suffering from a lack of attention, but I don't. It's impossible, because there's only two of us. I just get a little frustrated with the imbalance of things around here that's all.

It was Saturday morning, and I was staring out my bedroom window, watching the rain pelt down outside, dampening my already soggy mood. My mood was soggier than the sandwiches Mom puts in my

lunch, and that's saying something. The sky was hidden by an ominous veil of cloud, similar to the blanket of dread that hung heavily over my head. Soccer had been cancelled for the day due to dangerous conditions, so I was already down in the dumps to begin with. What's so dangerous about a muddy field I want to know. If you ask me, it only makes it more fun, sloshing around in the mud, trying to kick a ball that's heavier than lead. Having a mud bath in the pouring rain is pure awesomeness!

So, when Mom told me the dirty rotten stinkin' news, I exploded.

I continued to glare out the window, my eyes glazing over as my thoughts jumped between constructing and mining, fighting zombies, and farming carrots, to thinking about my mate Matthew's awesome gaming birthday party that I was *supposed* to be going to that night.

I imagined his party with heaps of candy and chips scattered around the motionless bodies of boys engrossed in a world of PlayStations and Xboxes. There would be no interruptions to ruin the video game marathon, except Matthew's Mom discreetly sneaking in with more food. I pictured the lounge room floor, layered with bodies, wall to wall, some lying on their back, others on their elbows, while Matthew, the birthday king, sat in the centre on his bean bag.

And right in the far corner, there'd be an empty spot where some poor, lost boy should have been, who didn't turn up. And that poor, lost boy would be me. And it's all because of my family. It's their fault that I wasn't going to be at Matthew's birthday bash, aka 'marathon video game all-nighter', 'super slayer smash up party'. Why me? WHY ME?????? Well I was determined to find a way to get to that party, even if I had to run away from home.

There was only one thing I could do to squash back the overwhelming anger and fury that was rising inside of me, taking over every cell like an enemy invading foreign terrain. There was only one thing that I knew that could conquer the strong feelings of doom.

I flipped open my laptop, and powered the machine on. I slammed my body onto my bed angrily, trying to get rid of the anger stuck in every atom. It felt so good, so I did it again, throwing myself violently through the air before I landed. It was exhilarating, and it brought back memories of jumping up and down on the bed like a trampoline when I was five. So I threw my shoes off, and began to bounce; at first tentatively, but then vigorously, reaching for the ceiling. I distinctly remembered my mom's voice echoing through the halls of history, "Get off that bed NOW! It's not a trampoline you know. You'll break the slats underneath, blah blah blah."

As if the bed would break, I thought to myself as a loud cracking

sound snapped from beneath me. I cringed as I looked under the bed, preparing myself for the worst. Two pieces of wood strayed jaggedly from each other until I carefully pushed the offending one back into position.

I gently climbed back onto the bed waiting for tell-tale sounds to give me away, but there was nothing. Relieved, I decided it would be a little secret between myself and the bed. No need for my mom to find out. I just had to remember to make my bed every morning so she didn't get too close to the incriminating evidence (not that she would ever be nice and make it for me anyway). I also had to remind myself that I was possibly twice as heavy as I was when I was five, and it was probably not a good idea to use the bed as a trampoline, or anger venting machine anymore.

After my bed breaking episode, the computer had finally booted up and I could forget all my troubles for a while by playing Minecraft. I logged on, lay back on my pillow with my knees up, and placed the computer comfortably on my lap ready to take on the zombies from the Nether. I knew as ugly and beastly as their boofy, square heads were, they were good for helping me forget about my annoying family and their crazy ideas.

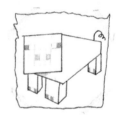

I jumped on in as soon as the game began and headed out to create a nether reactor. On completion, the grand portal looked amazing with its gold and iron glistening in the sunshine. I was actually quite proud of my efforts. I got in and ventured out to the Nether amidst the perilous barren land, bumping into a harmless pig on the way. "Come hither you pink pedestrian," I said aloud. "Come with me and make yourself useful or be minced into pink pork pie." I tamed it with a carrot, and it gladly joined me on the adventure.

Not long after, as I trekked through the dried grass, a group of Zombie Pigmen tried to overwhelm me by ganging up on me after I provoked their leader with my sword. I tried to fend them off by damaging them with TNT ignited with flint, but they became hostile towards me and their anger enraged. My adrenalin pumped fiercely as I returned the fury slashing my sword in every direction. I could feel my blood boiling inside me as I defended myself against the savage enemy.

I relished the chance to become lost in the perilous challenges of Minecraft. After the terrible news I had received from Mom that morning, it was the only thing that could help ease the pain. Not even the new 'Dragonball Z' Xbox game or 'Grand Theft Auto' could eradicate the thoughts of desperation.

Minecraft was the only way I could stay cool and not lose my sanity. I need Minecraft like I need oxygen; maybe even more than oxygen. It is a necessary part of my survival in this world.

In fact, I learnt this really interesting thing in the health lessons we have with Harold the dorky giraffe who rides around with a racy looking health teacher in a weird bus. There's this thing called 'Mambo's pyramid of needs'. Or maybe it's Manbo, or Maslow, I forget. At the bottom of the pyramid is the really important physical stuff that we can't live without, like water, oxygen and basic food. Whereas at the top is the less important, airy fairy stuff like love and self-esteem (that's when you love yourself), and probably candy. Well for me, Minecraft is right there on the ground floor level, sitting happily next to Oxygen and water in all their grand importance, keeping my heart and lungs ticking away nicely.

Amen to Minecraft peeps!

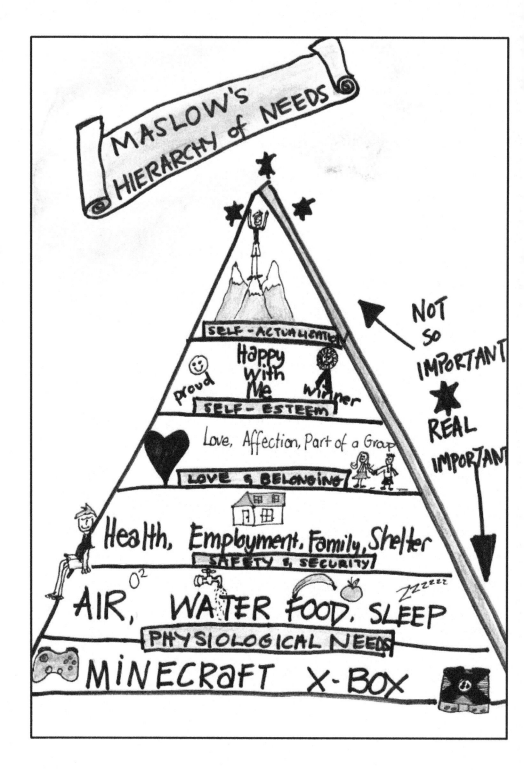

I'd nearly taken out all of the beasts when a high pitched whining sound infiltrated the action, causing my concentration to waver for a second, and the biggest and ugliest of them all slayed me to the ground, causing me to lose three hearts. The familiar whining sound came threateningly close and my unease grew with each closing sound.

"AGHHHHHHHH!" I yelled, as my door burst open. "Do you have to scream like that every time I'm going to massacre one of the pigmen?" I said. "And don't you know doors were made so polite people could knock on them?"

"Dad's home, Dad's home. I heard him toot in the driveway," Lisa said with uncontained excitement, completely ignoring my insults. Lisa was the person God put on this earth to make sure that I never had a good time. She also has the important duty of making sure Mom knows about everything I do wrong, *and* she plays a vital role in making sure my life is not a fun place. It's her job and she does it so well.

"So what!" I said, trying to disguise my curious excitement. Ever since Dad had said at the start of the week that he was bringing home a surprise on Saturday, I had been anxious to know what it was going to be. Every night that week, while I lay trying to sleep, thinking about Zombie Pigmen, creepers, aliens, Endermen and Ender dragons, the odd thought about the secret surprise would intercept my thoughts and hang around like a rotten fart smell keeping me awake all night.

Lisa on the other hand kept doing what she does best, and pestering Dad every day to find out what it was. Every day she would ask him the same questions like over and over again until I could see little smoke bombs of frustration escaping out of his earholes as he gave her the same answer over and over again. "I'm not telling you or anyone until

Saturday Lisa. Then you can see for yourself. Not even your Mom! All I can say is the whole family will enjoy it." Of course Mom would be in on the action, because I saw him wink at her.

I cringed when I heard Dad say that. Every time he says something's for the whole family, it has the potential to be disastrous.

"Oh come on Dad. Is it a dog?" Lisa had whined.

"Not telling."

"It's a dog isn't it? I knew it. We're getting a dog Ryan!" she had shrieked. "Dad's bringing home a puppy on Saturday."

Lisa was losing it, running around the house doing a happy dance. She looked like

such a dork, flapping her arms around like a zombie octopus, and doing this funny thing with her bum.

But I couldn't help get excited thinking that Dad must have given some signal away, and we really were getting a fluffy addition to the family again finally.

"Lisa!" Dad called out in a serious tone. "We are not getting a dog! How many times do I have to tell you? Dogs don't belong in this house anymore." Lisa's bottom lip dropped into a sulky pout.

"Why not? You're mean!"

"Watch your tone young lady. Just accept it."

"Well is it a putty tat?" she asked childishly.

"No!"

12

"A gold fish?"

"No!"

"A squirrel?"

"Doubtful."

"Hamsters?" Her voice was

starting to get real whiny. I mean more than usual.

"No, No, Nopey nope."

"Well, you know, this time I really would accept an ant, and I don't care if it *is* a green ant or a purple one with pink spots. It's time this family had a living pet so we can learn the responsibility of caring for something. That's what my teacher says anyway. They actually highly

recommend it. It's a fact. We're the only family that doesn't have a pet in the whole school you know."

Oh my sister!!! Does she know what she sounds like, ever? Have you heard what a peacock crossed with a crow on steroids sounds like? Well it sounds like a melodious symphony compared to my sister's whinging and whining. She goes on and on and on and on in that high pitched cackle.

Sometimes I wish Mom and Dad would pack her up and send her back to the baby making farm and ask for a refund, or at least exchange her for a silent model. Ever since her body went all weird and she

developed those bump things 'you know where', she's gone all crazy. One minute she's kinda ok and nice and all, then the next she's like psycho zombie meets Dracula meets Barbie.

"Lisa," Dad said in a serious drawn out tone, like he meant business. "Do you think you would mind carefully picking up your bottom lip, taking it up to greet your top lip and gently supergluing them together? Just for a day or so. We'll drip feed you if you get hungry."

"DAD!! You're so mean! Everyone's so mean to me in this family." Lisa stomped out with her bottom lip dragging on the ground in the biggest huff. Dad looked at me and winked before going back to his newspaper. I couldn't help laughing. I'm not sure Dad would win 'Father of the year' award for his comment, but gee it was funny. I couldn't help wondering **ALL** week what his surprise was going to be.

2. A Dark and Stormy Night

It all started one dark and stormy night. No it wasn't really, but I just wanted to set the scene as dark and gloomy. Because that's what the whole situation became when my mom and dad stuck their noses into my business and ruined my life once again.

The week had started off pretty awesome, but as each passing day went by, it slowly went downhill like a big fat turtle trying to snow ski down a mountain on a couple of shovels. I haven't actually seen one try, but I'm guessing it's a pretty dismal gig.

On Monday morning, Matthew, my best buddy met me at the front gate of the school with a big dumb smirk on his face. That didn't strike me as unusual because he always has a big dumb smirk on his face. Matthew is the one who I always said missed out on the brain delivery when God was handing them out for free, because he was too busy making fart sounds in his mommy's stomach. Yeah Matthew is always the fart felon in our class. He has been since the third grade when he started getting cheeky, and now in the fifth grade, he's king of the farts. And I'm not just talking about the squeaky underarm kind that he used to do. I'm talking about the real life blasters. He's a very gassy kind of kid, that's for sure.

I swear Matthew's Mom gives him baked beans for breakfast, lunch and dinner, seven days a week. He lets rip the worst honkers ever. He has a different kind for different times of the day; the silent kind, that are deadly in smell, the trumpet kind, that sound like they belong in the

15

London symphonic orchestra, and the squeaky, squelchy kind, that sound like they might contain something a little more than gaseous vapour. Eewgh, gross. Just thinking about those ones makes my stomach do somersaults.

Matthew's grin grew into a wide mouthed spectacle as I approached him. He reached into his bag and grabbed a dog eared envelope.

"What's this?" I asked, eyeballing the scruffy handwriting on the front. It had my name 'Ryan' on the front. I had forgotten, Matthew's birthday was approaching and I excitedly tore it open wondering what awesome party he would be having.

Matthew's parents were so cool with his parties. One year when we were little, we all got to sleep in the back yard in tents, and have a fire and toast marshmallows. Then the following year, we got to pitch the tents in the local park and sleep out. It was right across the road from his house so it wasn't such a big deal. His dad said we had to have the tents packed up by day light in case we got into trouble by the park police. But it was cool as. We spent the whole night awake on our portable games and told each other ghost stories.

The following year, we went to **Zone Ten**, which was topped the year after by **HOT SHOTS**. One year he invited me to Movie World for the whole weekend, and we stayed at this amazing hotel with a water park in the middle of the resort, and our room had a PlayStation built into the bunk bed. OMG! I thought I had died and gone to gaming heaven.

There I was, kicking back on the bed at night, head phones on, plugging into the coolest game **everrrrrrr**, after an awesome day on the rollercoasters and thrill rides.

It was so much cooler going with him than with my own family.

His birthday parties are always so much better than mine, and that's an understatement. When I turned three, we had a picnic in the back yard. When I turned four, we upgraded and had a picnic in the park. When I turned five, we had a picnic in another more exciting park. That one had swing sets. Whoopee do! When I was six, we regressed back to the backyard, but I got to invite real live friends instead of the stuffed teddy bears that Mom and Lisa used to set up everywhere. She had this notion that all I wanted to do for my birthdays was have teddy bear picnics.

When I turned seven, I had the most amazing birthday upgrade and we went to Maccas. It was so much fun, Mom decided we could do it for my eighth birthday *and* my ninth birthday. I'm sure she'd made the booking for my tenth one when I said to her, " I don't need a party this year Mom." I couldn't face another McDonald's party with screaming toddlers throwing

cheeseburgers at each other in the next party room again.

I ripped open the envelope as the bell rang.

"So can you come?" Matthew asked.

"Hang on, hang on," I said as I looked at the hilarious looking invitation. Even his invitations were cool. It was a graphically designed invitation with Matthew's head on a cartoon body doing all of his favourite things; playing Xbox and PlayStation, eating candy, stuffing his face with ice-cream and pizza all at once.

It was so funny. At the top of the page in bold writing it said **'ALL NIGHT GAMING MARATHON'**. My eyes lit up at the thought of gaming all night; something my mom and dad would **neverrrrrrrrr** let me do in my house, not even for my 21st birthday party.

"This is awesome! When is it?"

"Can't you read dummy?"

"Doh!" I said, realising the date was on the bottom. The party was that coming weekend so I didn't have long to wait. "Who's going?"

"Oh you know, just the gang. Josh, Jacob, Tom and your mate Nigel."

"NIGEL? You invited Nigel? What for?"

"Well it's my birthday, I can invite whomever I want."

"Yeah but.. but Nigel?" Nigel was the fifth grade meanie who just happened to be super good at computer games. He has also come up with the crazy notion that I'm his best buddy ever since I gave him the PS game I won at the start of the year in The PlayStation playoffs. The PlayStation Play offs was a competition our awesome teacher, Mr Higginbottom had for us at school, and I won, despite my family trying to sabotage my chances by absconding with me out of the country.

Nigel used to bully everybody, but since the competition he's sort of backed off a bit. I saw in a movie one day, that psychologists state that one of the reasons young boys bully, is because they have a little wiener. Every time I look at Nigel I think of that movie.

"Seriously? Is he going to come?"

19

"Nah, I'm kidding. I wasn't for real. I just said it to see the look on your face." Matthew burst out laughing, but he stopped when I punched him in the shoulder. "OW! What did you do that for?"

"Sorry, I was just kidding," I mimicked him. "I wasn't for real. I just did it to see the look on your face," I said with a smug look. "Ok, so this is going to be awesome. I can't wait for the weekend. So much good stuff is going to happen."

"Yeah?"

"Yeah. Dad's bringing home this awesome surprise home for every-one on Saturday."

"What is it?"

"Der! If I knew what it was, it wouldn't be a surprise."

SQUELCH! SPLAT!

"Matthew!" I whacked him on the shoulder again, pretending I was offended at his gigantic fart, as I laughed my guts out.

"That wasn't a fart, I just stood on a frog back there," and then he followed up with a deadly silent one.

PPPFFFFFTT!!

"Oh Pooo! You stink!" I laughed hysterically, as I side tracked away from him out of the danger zone. He laughed back at me and aimed his butt cheeks in my direction.

"Get away you stink monster," I said, as I threw my bag along the ground at him like a bowling ball. The bag landed a centimetre away from a tiny school girl who looked like she'd just stepped out of a carry cot. She looked at the bag as though it was a bomb about to blow up in her face. Then she ran away before it blew up.

I immediately regretted my decision to piff the bag when I saw a teacher in view. My heart immediately thumped into overdrive as I thought of the consequences. If the teacher saw me, I'd be in big trouble. If I was in trouble, I wouldn't get to play in the PlayStation club at the end of the week. And that was basically my whole reason for living. In fact, I think it was the reason God put me on this Earth. I quickly hung my head and kept walking as if nothing had happened, focusing on a trail of interesting colored stones. They suddenly became the most interesting stones I'd ever seen as I tried to block out the calls of the teacher.

"Sprung big time," Matthew taunted. "Looks like Rino won't be in the PlayStation club this week."

"Some friend you are," I whispered under my breath as I kept walking, leaving my bag festering in the dust as I gained pace and pretended not to hear the teacher call out as the school bell rang.

3. Sprung Big Time by a Dork

"Excuse me young man," a teacher whom I'd never seen before came after me as I got close to the school building. Or I should say, she stalked after me. I looked up with the cheesiest smile I could summons from my petrified body.

"Yes Miss."

"I think you may have left your bag back there."

I tried to look dumb, which unfortunately (or fortunately) doesn't come easy for me, as I like to think that I am a pretty smart kid. Matthew on the other hand, well he has to work hard at not looking dumb, even though he's actually smart sometimes, when he wants to be.

"Ah no, I don't think so," I answered. She must have thought I was the village idiot direct from Minecraft village. There I was, no bag on my shoulder heading into class, a lone bag sitting smouldering in the dust ten metres away, with a vivid memory of some kid scooting a bag along the ground.

YEP! I was in trouble! I'd never seen this person before, so I hoped she wasn't a teacher. Maybe she was just a mom going to work in the cafeteria.

She walked right up to me with an unsympathetically stern face; something that resembled a tyrannosaurus rex on a bad hair day.

Yep! She was definitely a teacher, and yep, I was definitely in for it. Big time! My heart sank to the bottom of my feet. Actually I think it went so low, it slimed out of my feet and was stomped on by all the kids running past to class. That's how squashed I felt, now that I knew I would probably miss out on the PlayStation club. Bummed out on the first day of the week. Big time loser, that was me. I could see the world caving in before my eyes, an event worse than a nuclear disaster looming perilously close.

No PlayStation club = The world is over!

I hung my head low imagining the look on Mr Higginbottom's face when he heard I had been in trouble. His look of disappointment would be nothing compared to the pain and torture I would be feeling in my heart. Surprisingly, it wasn't because I wouldn't get into the club, but because I found myself not wanting to disappoint *the* best teacher in the world. He was such a cool teacher despite his unfortunate name. I mean seriously, how many teachers that roam this Earth bring PlayStations to school? Bet you can count them on one finger!

"Well I think you'd better scoot on over there young man, pick up that bag for whomever left it there, and get to your class."

I looked up in astonishment. *Was that it? Was that all she was going to say? She didn't even ask for my name.*

"What's your name?" SPLAT! There went my heart again trampled on the ground, just as it was trying to crawl back into its cosy spot. I thought of saying 'Matthew' but not even I could be that low.

"Ryan," I sheepishly replied.

"Well Ryan. It's been nice meeting you. My name is Miss Dorklands. Perhaps I will see you again sometime."

'Thanks, but no thanks,' I said inwardly, in my mind, but outwardly I said, "Yes Miss," as I ran off toward the bag feeling extremely relieved and giggling to myself. 'Dorklands!!' What sort of name was that? Did she come from some sort of land where dorks lived? That was hysterical. She was going to be on the wrong end of a few cruel jokes from her students that was for sure. I couldn't wait to tell Matthew what had happened, but he had gone. Some friend he was.

4. Where is Mr Higginbottom?

I grabbed my bag which seemed to have a dusty layer covering my Dragon Ball Z emblem, and ran to the classroom. I didn't want to be late. Mr Higginbottom had this thing about everybody being on time. He says 'punctuality is the courtesy of princes'. I have no idea what he means by that, but when I asked my dad, my dad laughed and said, "rubbish, punctuality is the virtue of the bored. And the problem with being punctual," he added laughing, "is that no-one is ever there to appreciate it, because *everyone* is always late!" I don't really understand what either of them were going on about, but I guess my dad doesn't have the same beliefs as Mr Higginbottom. Even so, I still like to remain punctual for Mr Higginbottom's class because it's polite *and* I don't want to get into trouble, and miss out on the PS club.

As I approached the class I could see the door was shut, and it looked like the other kids were already inside. *Bummer. I was late.*

This day was not working out how it was supposed to. My heart started racing like a horse with muscles on steroids, running around a racing track, as I quietly opened the door.

The other kids were sitting on the mat quietly facing the front. I couldn't see Mr Higginbottom so I thought I had a second chance of skulking in quietly undetected.

I put my bag at my desk and as I turned around to head for the mat, this unimaginable creature stood above me, looming down at me, like a ghastly apparition, appearing from nowhere, waiting to pounce. This time my heart wretched up into my throat like I was going to barf, waiting for the inevitable.

"We meet again Ryan." It was the bag lady. "I hope you don't make a habit of being late to your classes. I always say punctuality is the virtue of princes. Please sit down on the mat with the rest of your class who chose to be punctual." What is it with all these teachers and princes? Haven't they had a good look around at their classes lately? There are definitely no princes to be found for miles around here. Maybe a couple of wannabe princesses in my grade though.

I gave Matthew a puzzled look as I placed my butt cheeks next to him on the mat. I raised my eyebrows up and down at him to get some answers. But typical Matthew had on his dumb face and had no idea what I was trying to say. He probably thought I had a bug in my eyebrow and was trying to twitch it out of there. I really hated sitting on the mat. It made me feel like we were back in the first grade. The only time Mr Higginbottom ever made us do it was when he was announcing who got in the PlayStation club at the end of the week.

I looked around at the others to see if anyone could give me the low down, but everyone was sitting really still and really quiet as if they were frightened or something. I was hoping Mr Higginbottom would appear soon so the bag lady, whoever she was, could show us her magic skills and do a quick disappearing act. I had this really bad feeling about her.

"Right class, as I was saying before Ryan decided to join us, my name is Miss Dorklands and I will be your teacher for..."

WHAT? WHAT was I hearing? My head went all fuzzy and the room started to spin. I stuck a finger into my ear and tried to remove the obvious build-up of goopy ear wax. I must have heard incorrectly. For a moment I thought she said she was our teacher. In my head I visualised myself kneeling down and I began to pray. I don't pray very often, well alright, hardly ever. In fact, I never pray, but right then, I prayed to the Gods, the moon, the sun, the fairies, anything that would listen. "Pleeeeeease bring Mr Higginbottom back after lunch dear God. I know I'm sometimes a bit cheeky to my mom, and well, ok, my dad too, but I won't be anymore. I promise I won't play Minecraft under the sheets at night when Mom thinks I'm asleep, and I won't drink all the lemonade and refill the bottle with water anymore. I even promise to stop putting worms inside Lisa's bed at night. I'll do all that stuff if you could please just bring Mr Higginbottom back and get rid of this lady who doesn't like boys throwing school bags. She looks mean. Please God."

"Ryan! Ryan." The sound of my name interrupted my prayers. What sort of teacher interrupts someone's prayer? I could tell already she was evil. "Ryan, would you mind listening in to what I'm saying. I hope I'm not going to have any trouble with you. This is the third time in twenty minutes I've had to speak to you. It doesn't make for a good start to the week now does it?"

"Sorry Miss, I just felt dizzy for a minute." I heard Matthew snigger behind me and I felt Josh dig his finger into my back, rubbing it in, that I was in trouble. I never get into trouble, but I was still trying to come to terms with the fact that Mrs Bag lady had said something about being here all week. Would that mean…? Could that mean………?

27

5. The Wicked Witch of Dorklands

"Yep! That's what it means," said Matthew as he batted the handball back to me during morning break. And it's not only this week, but next week as well, and every week for the whole month."

"WHAAAAAT? A whole month. Nooooooo. This can't be happening."

"I know. It sucks right," agreed Matthew. "There's no way she'll let us do the PlayStation club."

"She probably doesn't even know what a PlayStation is. She probably thinks it's a play list at a radio station or something. Where is Mr Higginbottom anyway? Did she say anything about him?"

"No, she just said she would be teaching us for the whole month."

"The whole month!" I felt like swearing, but swearing's not cool. I think it just makes kids look like they're trying to be tough. "Maybe he went and got married and now he's on his honeymoon."

The thought of Mr H kissing Miss Egbutt gave me the creepy crawlies. When I get married, I'm going to marry someone that likes Minecraft, PlayStation and XBOX. We can spend our honeymoon sitting on 'his and her' deck chairs, playing Minecraft together on separate computers. EEWWGHH! Just the thought of getting married gives me the heebie jeebies.

"No, Miss Egbutt's here. I saw her getting a coffee at the cafeteria before school. Unless he dumped her and got married to someone else. That would be a pity 'cos then there won't be little butts and bottoms running around when they have babies." Matthew laughed hysterically at his own joke about their names. No-one even really knew for sure

28

whether they were in love or not. Everyone just made jokes about it all the time because they shared the same office, and they both had bums in their surname.

"I know what's happened," Josh butted in, (talking of butts) as he ran up to us. He'd been at his violin class and was always late to morning break on a Monday, which was really annoying because we wanted him to play handball with us. Josh is an awesome handball player. That's because he's awesome at everything he does; Minecraft, PlayStation, XBOX, and he's pretty awesome at school work too.

When God was handing around brains, I think he gave Matthew's share to Josh, because Matthew was too busy farting in his Mommy's tummy somewhere and missed out. We always tease Mattie about that. He doesn't care though.

"You know where Mr Higginbottom is? Whatever it is, it can't be as important as teaching us," I said.

"You mean, letting us play the PlayStation at school," added Matthew.

"Yeah well, that too. Where is he Josh? Spit it out."

"My Mom said his Mom is sick and he's gone to look after her."

I'd never really thought of Mr Higginbottom as having a family, and a mom. When he comes to school every day, he's just Mr Higginbottom, and on Fridays when he comes with his big, black brief case containing PlayStations and games, he is 'awesome' Mr Higginbottom. I started to feel a little bit guilty that I'd said nothing could be as important as coming to school. But I soon forgot my sympathy when the bell rang, and I started panicking about going back into class with the wicked witch of Dorklands.

"Oh no! Now we have to go and face that ogre again. She'll probably makes us do algebra all the way through to lunch time."

"What's wrong with her? I think she's nice," Matthew said in her support. Some friend he was. Didn't he remember how she tormented me over the bag incident?

"You saw how grumpy she was at me when I just gently threw my bag on the ground. Probably on a power trip 'cos it's her first day."

"RINO! Are you for real? You piffed your bag straight at me ten meters along the ground, and it nearly bowled over a toddler, and she sprung you. Then, instead of reporting you, she asked you to pick it up.........nicely. What are you going on about?"

"Some friend you are; sticking up for a teacher. You're just trying to suck up to her because she's new."

"She's ok Rino," Josh agreed. What was this? Stick up for teachers day or something? I think she must have put them under a curse or something.

"Now class, I have some good news for you, something I hope you will all enjoy," she began, after making us sit on the smelly mat again. "Instead of doing blackboard work all day, every day, I'm going to break it up with a fun competition each day with a final on Friday." My ears pricked up. This was starting to sound very interesting. Maybe she wasn't such a bad teacher after all. Maybe Mr H had given her the low down of how this classroom works, and why most of us get awesome results. I had this crazy feeling inside that she was about to surprise us with the same deal, and that she would carry on with the PlayStation club. Things were starting to look up............I hoped anyway.

6. Running SUX

I looked over at Matthew and nudged him. He winked at me which meant he was thinking the same thing as I was. My body did this massive sigh as relief flooded all my veins knowing that Mr Higginbottom had set up the PlayStation club with Miss Dorklands before he left. He didn't desert us at all. Life was good again.

"So," she began, with a big cheesy grin on her face, suddenly appearing less of the monster that she was, "after lunch every day, when your mind is feeling drained from all the exciting learning, your legs are feeling puffy and tired from sitting all day, and you're wondering how you're going to make it until the bell, we are all going to jump up, reach for the sun, and go outside and run, run, run. Then, when we think we can't run any further, we're going to run some more until our heart rates are pumping, and our bodies feel exhilarated.

SPLAT! THUD! KAPLOP! That was the sound of my heart plummeting to the ground at the sound of the word run. Running and me just didn't get along well together. My heart rate was pumping at the mere thought of running circles around the oval. I didn't have to *do* the run to get that happening.

"And on Friday," she said, her face gleaming as though she was making some million dollar announcement, "we are going to have a running competition to see who's been training the hardest. I might even provide a little prize." She looked around the classroom as though she were the queen handling out golden nuggets to her villagers.

But instead of excited cheers, she was greeted with stunned faces, shocked beyond belief. What did she expect us to do? All bow graciously at her mercy? Jump up and shout, "Yippee! We get to massacre ourselves into exhaustion every day RUNNING!!" Not likely.

Running was reserved for cross country days and athletic carnivals where you were physically and mentally bullied into competing by the PE teacher. I think I would prefer to stay and do a double dose of algebra after lunch each day than go running. Running was for wannabe Olympians, not for normal kids like me, and Matthew and Josh.

I looked over at Josh whose betraying eyes were gleaming at the idea. Of course I should have known, Josh was awesome at running too. He loved it. But then, his legs were made of muscles. My mom said my legs were made out of lead, so he had an advantage.

Seriously, how could she compare the two; PlayStation competition versus a running competition? Ah, like, there's no comparison. One will get kids working hard, and one will get kids running; in the OPPOSITE direction, never to return.

There was just no comparison, and absolutely no sense in her way of thinking. I could see this was not going to be a good week. Thank goodness for Matthew's party at the end of the week. It was going to be the life saver that pulled me through. Knowing that I had that to look forward to would be the thing that kept me pumping every vile step I took around that forbidding oval.

Some of the kids had a bit of a moan, and some even bothered to ask if everyone had to do it. But Miss Dorkland's shocked response was very definite that we were all going to do it, and we were all going to benefit greatly from it.

"Before I've finished here, we are all going to be very fit sausages, and feel great for it. You might even be good competition for next year's Olympian runners," she laughed to herself.

Who ever heard of a fit sausage before? Who had even seen one? Most sausages I'd seen were full of dripping fat, so I was gobsmacked as to how they could be fit. This was going to be another teacher with crazy sayings.

At the end of the day, Matthew, Josh and I walked home talking eagerly about his party. Thoughts of Miss Dorklands and her running competition faded quickly into the background as soon as we left the school yard. I started thinking about what game I would play when I got home. I was allowed gaming time only on Mondays and Fridays (after my home work was finished of course) though sometimes I snuck in an extra session when Mom thought I was doing homework.

Jacob, one of my other friends joined us and we all talked the whole way home about Minecraft, and what we were going to build, and stuff. But when I got home, my plans were thwarted. As usual, there was a drama surrounding my family, and with darkness fast approaching, I WAS NOT HAPPY when I got home.

7. Home Alone

When it comes to my family, if there's something to go wrong, it usually does, and it's *always* Lisa's fault. I don't know why, but it *always* has something to do with her.

When I got home, the front door was locked which is not unusual so I knocked. No answer, so I knocked again; still no answer. I went around the back to get the spare key which Mom leaves out if she has to work. Mom works in the kitchen at the local hospital. She says she's a food technician, which is just a glorified kitchen hand. Mom says she had to have twenty years of cooking experience in kitchens before she could get that job. The only other kitchen I know she's worked in, is our kitchen at home.

When I looked under the secret pot plant…no key. All the windows and doors were locked because Dad keeps the place like a fortress, like he's waiting for an attack.

I ran back and forth in a frenzy looking for an opening or a sign or something. This had never happened to me before, and I told myself there was plenty of daylight left so I didn't have to get scared of zombies or weirdos.

I was definitely going to nominate my mom and dad for 'best parents of the year' award after this. I went back outside to see if Mom was driving up the road. As far as I knew she wasn't supposed to be working. I didn't have a phone because they reckon I'm not old

enough to have one, even though they think I'm old enough to loiter on the streets when I come home to an empty house.

I sat outside on the front porch for nearly an hour thinking of all the things that might have happened to them, and of all the things that might happen to me if I stayed out there alone in the night.

Finally, Dad and Lisa drove up, and as soon as Lisa saw me, sitting on the steps, she started laughing. As soon as I saw her, I started fuming. This was all her fault, I could just tell.

"Dad! Where's Mom? I'm locked out. I've been sitting here for an hour, and I'm freezing and I'm starved. This is child abuse. I could report you." Lisa was becoming hysterical laughing her head off evilly. "And it's probably *your* fault!" I said to Lisa, giving her one of her evil stares back.

"Now I thought Mom would have sorted something out for you buddy. She got called into work because someone was sick," Dad said all cheerily.

"Well she sent me a text checking that *I* had a key. Looks like she didn't care about you," the wicked witch Lisa taunted.

"What? Daaa'd!"

"I'm sorry son, I don't know what goes on, I just do as I'm told. You know the saying, 'Happy wife, happy life'. Lisa text me asking me to pick her up, so I did, and we had to do a delivery on the way home."

"So Mom didn't know you were picking Lisa up?"

"Well…. I guess not. I don't know."

"What about me? What was I supposed to do?"

"Well……I don't know," he replied vaguely. "Anyway, everything is all ok now, so let's move on"

"But it's not fair. It's scary being here not knowing if anyone is ever going to come home, not knowing if your family is still alive or if they've been attacked by mutant aliens and sent to another planet." Secretly I was thinking that wouldn't be such a bad idea in Lisa's case.

"Get over it, sooky bubba. Goo goo ga ga."

"Get lost evil witch."

"Now you'll probably have nightmares tonight about being 'home alone' in a dark deserted house with spooks and ghoulies."

"I can deal with nightmares. I deal with you every day don't I? And you're the worst nightmare ever," I snapped back.

"Come on son, how about I give you some free computer time to make up for it?"

"DAD! Seriously, Monday '*is*' my computer day!"

"Well how long do you get?"

I was about to say an hour which is what I *do* get, but somehow, "one and a half hours," slipped out before I could stop it.

"Ok how about two hours for tonight, and don't tell your Mom. And don't forget to do your homework before we have tea."

"Sure Dad, sounds fair." I didn't think Dad needed to be reminded that the rule was that I did my homework first.

I threw my bag on the bench, ran into my bedroom and booted up the computer. Then I remembered I was starved so I went back to the kitchen to grab a snack. There was a note on the bench from Mom. My mom is a note writer. Everything she wants to say is written in dot form on a pink bit of paper with puppies on the top. And every dot has the words 'do this, do that, do this, do that' after it. It's always what we have to do. Sometimes I just wished I was a zombie with zombie parents and I wouldn't have to 'do' anything all day, except sleep and go out at night and scare villagers. And if I got locked out of my house I could just blow it up, to get in. Life would be so much easier.

I looked at the note to see if she'd said what was for afternoon tea, but she hadn't. She just said she'd had to rush off to work. Then she had the nerve to write on the note,

Ryan, Lisa has the key, she'll be home same time as you.

Great Mom! That's just brilliant, leaving a note for me inside a locked house and giving the key to Lisa who was never coming home anyway. I really needed a phone. It sucked that Lisa could have one and I couldn't. I don't know what makes her so special, just because she's older than me.

I looked in the cupboard, but the cupboard was bare. I was going to have to start calling Mom Old Mrs Hubbard with the bare cupboard. No cookies, no cakes, no chips, no pretzels, BUT OF COURSE THE FRUIT BOWL WAS OVERFLOWING.

I had a hunt for Mom's secret stash. She always keeps the good stuff hidden in unusual places like cereal packets and flour canisters. Once I even found a packet of candy in a box of snail pellets in the shed. The snails would love those. I wonder if candy would have the same deadly effect on snails as the pellets did. *And* I even found a packet of chocolate biscuits in her undies draw once. Gross! I didn't eat those!

I finally found a new jar of chocolate  spread that I didn't know Mom had bought, hidden behind the spice rack. There was some fresh bread as well. YUMBO! I opened the jar and to my horror, I wasn't the first person to open it. There it was, a fresh layer of smooth and creamy chocolate heaven with a big finger mark entrenched in it. YUK! That is soooo gross! I couldn't bear the thought of Mom dipping her finger into the chocolate spread. I put the jar away and sliced a banana. On the bright side, at least there weren't two finger prints double dipped in it.

"Dad, Matthew's party is on this weekend," I yelled out, not knowing where Dad was. "I'll be going ok?"

"Sure thing son," a voice came from somewhere. Dad never really listened to what I was saying. He always just agreed with everything. If I said, "Dad, do you mind if I lock Lisa away in a cupboard for two days without water and food?" Dad would just say, "sure thing son." He's pretty easy going, my Dad. It's my Mom who's the scary one. But I knew as long as I did all my chores at home and didn't get into any trouble, there would be no problem going to Mattie's party.

I kicked my shoes off, and jumped on my bed with my banana sandwich and my computer and bunked down for two hours of pure bliss. Just me, the banana sandwich and Minecraft. What more could a boy want? (Except maybe a chocolate spread sandwich).

In the game, I found myself sprinting off in a hurry to my tree farm, but unluckily, I tripped and fell into a hole which lead to a natural cave. Dodging the furious bats was hard enough, but not as frightening as when a monster spawner appeared, spawning zombies all over the place. My heart started racing as I quickly broke the spawner with my nearly broken iron pickaxe and slayed the zombies with my iron sword. With not much time to spare, I quickly gathered up some rare crafting materials; two ink sacks, three gold ingots, and four obsidian.

I started to feel a bit more relaxed enjoying the game, when all of a sudden out of the blue, I was confronted by this ginormous spider, two zombies and a skeleton charging towards me. What could I do? Swiftly, I knocked them into a nearby pool of lava where they died a painful death, smouldering on the burning fire.

I blocked up the lava, which stole the glow of the cave, so a blanket of darkness shrouded the game. As I roamed around the cave anxiously, I placed torches upon the walls so I could see, and then I spotted it. Could it be? Was it a diamond? As I approached it in excitement, my heart dropped when I saw it was just the boring lapis lazuli which resembled a diamond. Agghhhhhhh! I closed my laptop in frustration.

8. Torture School Concentration Camp

The rest of the week at school was torture, like living in a concentration camp. Every day was a mind numbing blur of Maths sums, spelling and running. By Friday, my legs felt like they were made of lead and that I had run over to Ethiopia and back EVERYDAY. They were overworked, exhausted and completely incapable of going another step. My body had probably lost so much weight from all the running that I possibly looked like I lived in Ethiopia. (Apparently, Ethiopia is a third world country where kids don't get to eat much and they get sick. Mom tells me about it when I get fussy over my food.)

As the rain started to pour down during our lunch break, I excitedly hoped that the big running competition final would be cancelled. My rain dance the night before had worked. Josh, who was the favorite to win, began to get disappointed.

"I hope we still get to race this afternoon," he said, "I've been training real hard."

"What? Seriously? You want to drag yourself around the oval like a drowned rat in gumboots?"

"Yeah! It will be cool. It will cool us down when we get hot."

"Yeah, whatever ya reckon' Josh."

"Yeah whatever," Matthew agreed. He wasn't really into running either, unless it was for soccer. Both Matthew and Josh were on my soccer team. Dad calls us 'the three soccerteers' instead of the three musketeers.

"Well I want to win the prize anyway."

"Wow Josh. It's a chocolate bar. Awesome prize. NOT! When Mr Higginbottom puts up a prize, it's a new PlayStation game. When Miss Dorkie puts up a prize, it's a neeeeew chocolate bar," Matthew said in a funny voice like he was a game show host. That's the other thing about Matthew. He does these crazy different voices all the time and mimics everybody, like Mr Higginbottom. Oh I missed Mr Higginbottom.

The only different voices Miss Dorklands has is, boring, stern, grumpy and full on '*ANGRY*' reserved for special occasions.

After the bell rang, we all squashed in under the cover in front of our room trying to escape the falling sky waiting for Miss Dorklands to open the door. The smell of stinky kid's body odour combined with stale farts and wet woollen jumpers intermingled to produce a lovely after-lunch aroma. It gently wafted up my nostrils, causing my guts to violently puke (internally). I was so tormented by the ghastly smells, I felt certain I would have to go to the sick bay and rest. What a shame I would have to miss out on the world's most pathetic running competition.

A sneaky smile began to creep over my face as I pictured Miss Dorkland's reaction when I told her I was overcome with nausea and vomiting, and that I was devastated but I would have to miss the race. I would then say that I could try and start the race and hope that I wouldn't have to leave in the middle to puke violently on the side. Miss Dorklands would turn her nose up, cringing in disgust, and immediately send me to the sickbay, where I would pull out my computer magazine, put my feet up on the banana lounge with an unneeded sick bucket by my side, and suck on an icy cold lemonade. It was the plan of masterminds. I looked smugly around at Matthew who was getting shoved by Nigel standing behind him, pretending that he was squashed but relishing the chance to do a bit of body slamming.

"Hey back off Nige," I yelled. For some reason, ever since I kindly donated my PlayStation playoff's prize to Nigel, he seemed to listen to me, even though he does hang around like a bad fart too much.

"Hey, I can't help it. I'm getting shoved by Elysa," Nigel replied. Elysa was tiny and no way she could shove Nigel. He was full of it!

"Psst Matthew. I'm getting out of the run."

"What? How?" he replied.

"For reasons I can't control," I laughed.

"What are you talking about? I want to get out of it too," he said hopefully.

"Stop being lazy bums," Josh piped in. "Just enjoy it. It will be good fun."

"Yeah about as much fun as getting nailed by a whole troop of Minecraft Zombies on a rampage."

"What! Getting nailed by zombies is fun," Matthew added.

"Yeah I guess," I agreed. "Ok, well running is about as much fun as watching my sister do a dance concert. In fact I think I'd rather watch the dance concert. Now you know how much I hate running."

"Sssh! She's coming," goodie goodie Josh said. He wouldn't want anything getting in the way of him winning the grand chocolate bar. I began to put on my sick face, and started to look ill as though I'd just stepped off a cruise boat, overcome with sea sickness. I began to heave just to make the visual scene look really realistic.

"Ryan, what on earth are you doing?" Sarah, one of the big mouth girls said. "You look like you're a cat having an epileptic fit."

"Mind your beeswax," I snapped back at her, and went back to my heaving.

"Oh gross," a few of the girls added. "Get away from here. Go and practice your zombie ballet somewhere else."

Miss Dorklands arrived and totally missed me and my chucking in her rush to get out of the rain.

"Quickly boys and girls, let's get inside." Maybe I wouldn't have to put on my fake sickness. If Miss Dorklands was this worried about getting a little bit wet, then there was no way she'd have us running around like idiots in the rain.

SPLAT! KAPLOT! BOOM! That brain wave idea exploded when she added, "we'll just go and sit down inside and wait until the rain eases. We might have a quick Math's quiz while we wait."

GROOVY BABY! A Math's quiz. What more could a boy want as a warm up to a marathon? This woman was getting more and more like an army sergeant every day. But of course my mate Josh had to sing in my ears, "YEYY! A Math's quiz. Awesome!"

Of course Josh just loved Math's quizzes because he always won. Not only was he good at everything, he was good at Maths as well. BORING. Sometimes I wondered why we were such good friends when we were so different. He was good at everything, and brainy. Matthew and I were average at everything, and, well, not so brainy. But Matthew and I worked hard at  school, and that was the main thing my Mom always said. And she should know because she's a mom and moms know everything; well they think they do anyway.

Just as Miss Dorklands had wished, after the Maths quiz was over, the rain started to ease and there was actually a bit of sunshine teasing the low-hanging clouds threatening to dominate.

Time to get seriously sick. It was my only escape route. I was about to start faking my vomiting again when a terrible thought occurred to me and threatened to destroy all my well thought out plans.

AGHHHHHHHHHHH !!

9. Killer Teacher on the Loose

Matthew's party was the next day. The thought of it was the only thing that would keep me alive as we trudged around the oval tortured by 'Sergeant Dorklands Sir' in the running final.

The terrible thought I had, was, if I was sent to the sick bay, my parents would have to be contacted, and knowing my Mom, if she thought I'd been vomiting at school, she would put me into lock down mode at home. That meant, no visitors, no outings, no contact with human life, probably no food, no fun and definitely NO PARTIES. She'd probably even make me wear a mask over my mouth, and if she was in a really generous mood, she might let me breathe.

Because she works at a hospital where people hand round germs like candy, she's a bit over paranoid about the transmission of bad dudes that jump from skin to skin (germs). She's like the hand washing police.

She's always been pretty cautious, but when she bought home a lovely little diarrhoea (runny poo) bug one day, she went ballistic with the hand washing from then on. She said she never wanted to go through that unspeakable experience again. If it was so unspeakable, I don't know why she had to speak about it. I would have been quite happy not to hear about those sorts of stinky experiences.

Dad had stirred Mom up real bad when she had diarrhoea. When she was sitting on the toilet, he said to her, "I hope it's not hereditary love. I would hate for it to 'run' in the family." Then he got on a role with his diarrhoea jokes while poor Mom was sitting there trying to be quiet, but in reality it sounded like there was a steam train on steroids running through the bathroom.

45

"Hey love. Why did the girl take toilet paper to the party?"

"Go away!" was Mom's answer in between farts.

"No, wrong answer, because she was a party pooper."

"GO AWAY!" Mom repeated, starting to get really angry.

"Ok. I'm going. But do you want me to go and get some prunes? It will give you a good 'run' for your money," Dad chuckled hysterically at his own gross toilet humor as he left Mom in peace (except for the explosions). Eewgh! Dad is so gross when he's trying to be funny. And Mom is so gross when she gets a tummy bug!

Those ghastly memories from the bowels of my mind (hee hee) dredged up a time in my life that I would be happier to forget; though the sounds of my Mom exploding in the bathroom are heavily stuck in my mind unfortunately. And I'm sure the experience was imprinted on her mind as well, and I knew any suggestion of me vomiting at school, would dredge up all those violent memories for her.

Yep! It would be lock down for me, not to mention bucket loads of disinfectant lovingly tipped around my bedroom. Now that's enough to make anyone vomit. Lockdown would mean the whole weekend and that meant missing Matthew's party.

My heart sank, slowly at first, but then it went into a full on bungee jump and crashed onto the ground splattering into a million microscopic pieces of blood and guts, as I realised that I would *have* to do the stupid grand final running competition after all.

There was no way out of this nightmare. I looked for an escape route quickly out of the room, but there was nothing, unless I could grab onto the rafters, tarzan swing from beam to beam and catapult in a sling shot out the window. Or I could just stand up and declare to the teacher that I was exiting the building pronto.

Either way, I didn't think she would take too kindly to my ideas, so I sat on the mat and sulked, while Josh sat beside me beaming; proud of his winning effort on the Maths quiz, and no doubt proud of his winning effort that was about to arise in the running comp.

"Right children, I want you all to stand up and do three different types of leg stretches while I go and get ready," Miss Dorklands commanded.

Agghh! 'Children'. Who did she think we were? Kindy kids? I much preferred it when Mr Higginbottom called us kiddie widdies. And what did she need to go and get ready for? Ready for what? To stand on the surrounds of the oval with her whip and beat us into action?

I'd only got to my second leg stretch, because I kept falling over when Miss Dorklands came back. She'd changed into some sort of costume. I'm not sure who, or what she was supposed to be, but she looked like a pink flamingo, dressed in a pink singlet and black leg things with a pink sweat band around her forehead and wrists. I'm not really sure if she thought she looked good or if she was trying to be funny, but judging by the murmurs and sniggering coming from the class, I wasn't alone in my thoughts.

But she had awesome runners on. I reckon they would have been worth two hundred bucks. *She wasn't seriously going to run in the race? She couldn't. She wouldn't. She's a teacher, she's a lady and she's old.* Old teachers don't run. Especially old lady teachers.

Do they? I'm not sure how old she was, maybe even nearly thirty. It just didn't seem right. Unless she was just dressing up to get us in the spirit.

"Right, has everyone done their three leg stretches?" There were unconvincing murmurs all around, but no-one owned up to the fact that they hadn't done three.

"Ok Peter. What were yours?"

"Ah this one," he demonstrated, "and ahh......."

"Forgotten so quickly Peter? What about you Matthew?"

"Ahhh, I did a calf stretch, and a.....a....."

"You've forgotten already too. H'mmm. Who knows why it is important to stretch before running or any other vigorous activity?"

There weren't many volunteers, but Josh as usual had something intelligent to say. "Because it warms up the muscles."

"Yes that's right, and why is that good?"

"Well it's better to run when you're warm. I hate running when I'm cold," Matthew piped in with some totally unintelligent comment.

"Well.....I'm not sure that's totally correct, but possibly helpful. A warm-up helps increase the elasticity of your muscles and connective tissues, before putting them under stress, which makes them more relaxed and flexible. Running is just one example of an exercise that puts an enormous amount of stress on your body." Miss Dorklands spoke like she was a museum guide, giving us a tour of a muscle.

"What was that all about?" I whispered to Matthew. I had no idea what she was going on about. The only thing I got loud and clear was something about **'stress on the body caused by RUNNING'**. DER!!! And we all know that stress is bad for you and your heart, and stress can kill you. She was trying to kill us! She was a murderer. A killer teacher was on the loose. I could just see the newspapers and social media the next day. **'Killer teacher on the loose after massacring 25 students, torturing them to a painful death by too much exercise'.**

I screwed up my nose at the thought of the ensuing torture. Josh gave me a dig in the ribs and said, "Come on, this is going to be awesome. We get out of school work."

"She's trying to kill us," I whispered back.

"You'll be ok. Just stick with me."

"Yeah right! You going to piggy back me around?"

"Excuse me boys, is there something you need to share?"

"Yes Miss, I want to share with the class the fact that we are in the hands of a mass murderer disguised as a flaming hot pink flamingo. I want to ask them if anyone has any bright ideas to implement a mass plan of escape before we are tortured." That was what I said in my head to myself, but out loud I said, "No Miss," and Josh answered quietly with his cheeks a burning shade of pink, "sorry Miss. I'm just excited about the race."

OMG! What a suck he could be sometimes. Luckily he is an awesome kid, otherwise I'd puke at his suckiness towards the teachers.

"Right then, good to hear. Let's get outside and finish our warm up. As we have all learnt, it's very good to have a warm up."

My worst nightmare had finally arrived. I was finally getting paid back for all the times I'd lied about who was eating the cookies out of Mom's secret stash, and for all the times I secretly had Minecraft under the blanket at bed time, and for all the mean things I'd done to Lisa. Actually, no, that was pretty fair because she does so many mean things to me; like the time she put prawns in my school bag on camp, and when she blamed the dog for putting dog poo in my shoe.

Just before the race began, it started to rain cats and dogs again. I'll never understand why people say 'raining cats and dogs' because I've never seen a cat or a dog rain out of the sky. Maybe it's because when the

rain comes down, it's like a dog is peeing on you. That's a pretty good reason to keep well under an umbrella if you ask me. I hoped Miss D would take pity on us, but of course her murderess streak took over and she went ahead with the race. But what I thought would be the worst twenty minutes of my life, actually turned out quite surprising.

You are not going to believe what happened. In fact, I was so gob smacked, I had to physically pick my jaw up from dragging it around the oval with me.

10. Stalked by the Dorkster.

I've never seen a pink flamingo in a running race, but when Miss Dorklands lined up at the starting line with us, she looked more determined and competitive than an Olympian reaching for gold.

"Yes that's right folks. Your biggest competition is me!" She laughed to herself and almost snorted. She had the weirdest laugh. "I want you all to try and keep up with me. I'm not the fastest. I'm not the best. I may even look a tad strange, but I have *courage* and *determination.* That's all I need to make it to the end, and that's all you need as well, *courage* and *determination* and a little bit of encouragement from your classmates."

I wondered how she would know who won if she was going to run, but as my thoughts rumbled around upstairs, the school principal started walking towards us. 'My savior,' I thought to myself. He'd found out about the unnecessary child cruelty that was happening to the fifth grade while Mr. Higginbottom was away, and he was coming to save us. Thank the stars.

"Ah, here he is now. Class, we are very privileged to have Mr. Robson take time out of his busy day to start our race for us and be here at the end to time it. Thank you Mr. Robson. That's very good timing."

"I wouldn't miss it for the world Miss Dorklands. I think it's a wonderful thing to see students so eager to improve their physical ability as well as their mind."

51

I put on the fakest smile I could muster when Mr. Robson scanned his eyes past me. I was trying hard not to grit my teeth at the same time.

"Good luck everyone," Miss Dorklands said.

"On your mark, set, and go," commanded the principal, and we were off. YIPEE! This day was something I had been waiting for all my life. **NOT!!!** I know we have school athletics carnivals and cross country and all that, but there was just something really rude about making us do more running during school.

"It's not fair," I said to Josh as we entered the second lap.

"Stop whining, just do it, and it'll be over soon. Stick with me."

"Yeah right. As if I can stick with you!"

"Well you're with me now aren't you?" He had a point. I was jogging along complaining to Josh the whole time, and I hadn't realized that Josh and I were running together, *and* we were in front. "And can you stop talking?" he continued. "It uses up too much energy."

"Hey wait up you guys," Matthew called from behind .

"Just do one of your farts Mattie, that will give you a super charged boost to propel you," I shouted back at him.

"DON'T YOU DARE MATTHEW!" said someone else.

I had this strange feeling come over me as I was running alongside Josh. It was a really bizarre feeling that I had never experienced before and it felt totally weird in my body, like some alien had overtaken me. I can't explain it but to say that I was *enjoying* running. Eeeek!! Did I just say that? My heart was thumping louder than a bass drummer, but I wasn't puffed out like I usually was. Maybe Miss super Dorkie's super training sessions had paid off and I was getting fit.

It was the first time ever that I had been coming first in a race (even if it was neck and neck with Josh.) I knew it wouldn't last and Josh would soon speed off when I began to tire, but I just wanted to enjoy the feeling of coming first while it lasted.

I kept waiting for Josh to take off and leave me, or for the others to catch up, but it wasn't happening. I looked over at Josh. He looked as tired as I felt, with puffed cheeks and sweat dripping off him in torrents.

"Hey why are you being so nice and running with me?" I said.

"I'm not being nice," he said puffing. "I'm just running."

"Yeah but you're stickin' with me."

"No, *you're* stickin' with me."

"You can go faster if you want. I'll be ok."

"No, actually I can't go faster. I'm running my fastest."

"Ya kidding right?"

"No I'm not and can you put a sock in your mouth? This answering a hundred questions thing is zapping my oxygen stores." Josh was gasping with each breath. Come to think of it, so was I. It probably *was* a good idea to just shut up and run. I looked behind us and to my amazement (and horror), Miss Dorklands was gaining on us. Here was this pink looking thing who was heaps older than us, catching up big time. 'That' was NOT going to happen. Not in my life time anyway. I was NOT going to be beaten by an old teacher, and a girl one at that.

"Come on Josh, let's go. Miss Dorkie is catching up to us." I started to speed up expecting Josh to level with me, but he didn't.

"You keep going then. I can't go any faster. I've got a bit of a stitch," he gasped.

"Great time to be getting a stitch Josh."

"Well I didn't exactly plan it to happen right now, sorry. Keep going, and STOP TALKING." I looked behind again and Miss Dorklands was closing the gap, stalking us, and she had this real mean look of determination on her face. It was just me, Josh and 'the Dorkster'. That's what some of the boys call her (not to her face). But right now, it seemed like a really good name for her in the biggest running competition this side of the universe. Ryan and Josh versus........ 'the Dorkster'.

"I'm not running any further without you Josh. Let's go. We can't let a teacher beat us. We've only got one lap to go." Victory was in sight as we both scrambled onto the final lap. I was absolutely smashed to pieces and yet I felt invigorated as though my legs could run faster than a speeding bullet, were more powerful than a locomotive, and able to leap tall buildings in a single bound. Yep, Superman had invaded my body and taken over, but I didn't care. Let him take it over if it helped me to beat the Dorkster.

My legs, though they were shattered, started to gain speed. The adrenaline surging round my body kicked in and masked the pain that had started to creep into my legs. I felt as though somewhere from deep inside, I could muster a sprint and bolt home through the cheering crowd of one.

As I started my brutal assault, I glanced behind to encourage Josh and I could see out of the corner of my eye, his body lamely buckling over into a heap and rolling spectacularly onto the ground. The favorite to win the race had just been struck off the board, and it didn't look good.

11. Energy Drink Catastrophe

"JOSH!" I screamed, not knowing what was happening to him. "Get UP!" I pleaded, as if our lives depended on it.

"Aghh," he groaned. "I have an evil alien inside me ripping my guts out."

"What?" I said as I jogged up and down on the spot. "Get up, there's an evil alien approaching us. We have to run."

"I can't. I have a stitch Rino. I've got the world's biggest stitch ever, so big, it would make the front page of the Guinness book of records. You go on. Hurry, you've got a chance to win. I just need to rest for a bit." He winced as he spoke, and his face resembled a dried up tomato.

I looked around and the rest of the group were catching up to us. Even Matthew was running solidly for him, probably propelled by a continuous supply of gaseous vapors.

"Go man!" ordered Josh.

"You be ok?"

"Of course. It's just a stitch. Go get that chocolate bar before Miss Dorklands wins it.

He was right. I had to win that chocolate bar. I couldn't let Miss Dorklands win it. That would be weird.

As I sprinted off with a renewed sense of energy, thinking about winning my first ever running race, I glanced behind to see the others getting dangerously close but all I could see was my mate Josh crawling to the edge, doubled over in pain. The others started to pass him, including the teacher who was now slowing up, but not one of them offered him help. Too busy thinking about their own chances, now that the favorite was out of the race. I looked at Mr. Robson at the finishing line cheering everyone on, and I looked at Josh in the other direction. My heart was torn between both, but my legs made the decision for me and without even realizing it, they did a full U-turn and headed back towards where Josh was laying. At the same time, Matthew pulled up alongside to see what was wrong.

"Give us a hand Mattie. He's not going to get out of this race so lightly."

"Huh?" said Matthew.

"You go one side and I'll go the other. He's run this far, he's going to make it to the finish line."

"Seriously guys, you don't have to do this," Josh said as we put his arms around our shoulders to support his weight, to take the pressure off his body.

"You waited for me at the start, so now I'm waiting for you at the end," I replied.

"Well you didn't wait for *me*," added Matthew cheekily, "but I'm still happy to help you out. I needed a break anyway," he said, still panting heavily. "Running is really not my thing. I much prefer the XBOX."

"Thanks guys. It's my own fault. I had an energy drink at lunch time. But I think I drank it too quickly."

"Yeah well, my mom reckons those energy drinks are dangerous. They've got too many chemicals in them."

"How does your mom know that?"

"I don't know. She thinks she knows everything about food because she's a food technician at the hospital. Actually she thinks she knows everything about everything."

They both laughed, and as we crossed the finish line, arm in arm finishing in.....last place, the rest of the class starting laughing too. I'm not sure if they were laughing at us or with us, or both, but we didn't care. I had expected to come last anyway. It was just a bonus that the three of us got to come last together, 'the three soccerteers'.

12. Finishing Last a Winner

After the race, we all flopped onto the grass. I was so exhausted I didn't even care about green ants, even though I'm paranoid of them. Most of the class was doing the same thing. I felt as though my insides had been rumbled around a washing machine one hundred times and then thrown into a stinking hot tumble dryer to finish.

But the funny part about it was, even though my body felt as though it were mummified, my mind was racing with excitement and triumph. Even though I came last in the race, I had actually been coming first for a while, and even more surprising, I was enjoying it. Sssshhhhhh don't tell anyone.

Miss Dorklands was really nice and said we could all just lay there quietly and bask in the glow of our achievements. Sounded like a nice idea, but rather than bask in a boring glow, whatever that was, we preferred to lie there and talk about Matthew's party coming up the next day. Matthew said there was going to be an awesome surprise as well as all the gaming and eating we were going to do. That really got us thinking, not to mention a tad bit excited. Knowing Matthew's parents, it was probably going to be something really neat. Instead of a party bag full of candy to take home, they were probably putting together a show bag full of PlayStation games. Maybe I was dreaming a bit on that one!

"What is it?" questioned Jacob.

"Ahhh it's a surprise," Matthew answered.

"Yeah, but what is the surprise?"

"Well if I tell you, it won't be a surprise."

"So? I don't care. I just want to know if I will like it."

"Don't worry, you will like it."

"Ah man, just tell us will ya!"

"No! My mom and dad said I wasn't allowed."

"So, do you do everything your mom and dad say?" Matthew was trapped on that one, because a lot of the time, he made up his own rules, *and* he got away with it; probably because he was an only child.

He was just about to tell us the exciting surprise when the rain started to get angry again and Miss Dorklands said it was time to go back to class, and to finish off the day, we were going to do something relaxing and easy. Sounded promising, but Miss Dorklands probably thought going for a 20 km run was relaxing.

13. Attack of the Zombie Pigmen

As I was lying in bed that night, my legs aching with tiredness and my feet feeling like they were pincushions, I was thinking about the race, and it suddenly occurred to me that I hadn't bought a birthday present for Matthew. I was going to jump out of bed and go and tell my mom, but I had a feeling of fear that if I tried to jump anywhere, I might not land. I didn't think my legs would ever be able to run again, let alone jump, or walk. It felt like someone had secretly cut out my muscles and replaced them with big round pieces of heavy iron ore.

I decided I would tell Mom first thing in the morning, as I lay in the bed drifting between slumber and hazy thoughts of PlayStations, XBOX games, Minecraft and birthday parties.

My eyelids had just about closed, when, to my horror, a creature resembling a Minecraft Zombie climbed in the window and headed towards me in the bed. His body was dripping with slimy goo, and his arm was bent up awkwardly behind its back, obviously concealing a deadly weapon to initiate his attack on me. My body froze and I squirmed under the covers while I held my breath and prayed to the lord above that he wouldn't notice me.

I even quietly gave him directions to Lisa's bedroom. My prayers went unanswered as further creatures; a pigman, an Endermen and several creepers all followed through the window carrying something behind their backs and headed toward my bed.

I felt like my eyes were bugging out of my head in total fear. As each of the evil monsters swung their arms around to fire at me, they started singing, "Happy birthday to you, happy birthday to you, happy birthday to Rino, happy Birthday you big poo." It was then that I noticed that none of them had guns, knives, axes, or anything perilous. To my shock, they were all carrying birthday presents wrapped in brightly colored paper, tied up with a string of leggo blocks. Weird!

I tried to tell them that it was Matthew's birthday, not mine, but they didn't listen. They just kept filing in through the window and loading me with birthday presents. I was enjoying opening all the exciting gifts when one of the ugliest creepers started to get violent. Party pooper! He pushed the others out of the way and grabbed me around the shoulders and started to shake me. I knew it was too good to be true. I knew Zombies and creepers didn't have a kind bone in their body. It was obviously all a ploy to 'betray me and then slay me'. His face was ugly and fierce looking and he was screaming at me, "Stop it. Stop it now!"

"Stop what? What am I doing?" I screamed in terror.

"Stop singing 'Happy Birthday' to yourself. It's not even your birthday. That's how up yourself you are."

I squinted as I tried to focus my eyes on the ghastly apparition. The moon light streaming in through the window played on its angry face, leaving vein like etchings all over. It was such an ugly sight.

"Stop it, do you hear me?" It kept repeating itself over and over, until finally my eyes focused on its ugly form.

"Aghhhhhh!" I screamed, when I realized it wasn't a Zombie but something far worse, far scarier, and far uglier.

"Get out of my bedroom Lisa!"

"Not until you promise to stop singing, or should I say, stop screeching. You woke me up!"

"Well *you* woke me up!"

"You woke me first!"

"Get out!"

"Do you promise to stop…."

"I wasn't singing."

"I know. You were screeching. You would give alley cats a bad name." I started to get out of my bed, glancing at the window as I pulled back the blankets, just to make sure nothing else was coming through. I began to chase Lisa out the door. She was so annoying. I think I needed to ask Mom and Dad for a lock on my door to keep zombies like Lisa out.

"I'm going. I'm going! Calm down."

After I'd rid my bedroom of the feral creature, I got back into the snuggly, warm bed, grabbed my tablet and began to play Minecraft. I wasn't really allowed to play in bed, but this was a special occasion. I had been terrorized by a monster (Lisa) and I would find it difficult to get back to sleep. That's the excuse I would give Mom if she sprung me anyway.

I lay there building my fortress and fighting off Endermen (real ones this time). As I drifted off to sleep I remembered that the following day was not only Matthew's party, it was also the day Dad was supposed to be bringing home the surprise. I was a little bit excited, but I was also a little bit anxious because every time Dad said he had a surprise, it was either really boring or really embarrassing.

Last time Dad said he had an exciting surprise for me, he showed up at school dressed as a pirate, with Mom dressed as a parrot. They turned up at assembly and sang stupid songs about sea shanties and did a very embarrassing skit from a pantomime that Dad was involved in. I was so embarrassed, I wanted a massive earthquake to erupt, and swallow me up in one huge gulp. How could they have done that to me? The worst part about it was, Mom blew me a kiss on her way down from the stage and then did a little "Rino wanna cracker" squawk. I have been mentally scarred for life from that torturous event. It took months before kids stopped saying "Rino wanna cracker," in the school yard.

I finally drifted off to sleep with my tablet lying on my stomach keeping me warm. When I awoke in the morning there was only 2 percent battery left so I quickly put it on charge before my mom came in. I didn't want her knowing I had been playing it before I went to sleep, and I didn't want her carrying on about the electrical waves that were probably penetrating my stomach all night and pulverizing my organs.

When I woke up my room smelt like a stink bomb so I guessed I might have let a few rip in the night. I didn't need to look out the window to know that the weather was horrid again.

I could hear the rain pelting down on our tin roof. It sounded like there was a herd of elephants rampaging across the top of our house; not that I've ever actually heard elephants racing on a roof. Funny about that! I heard a

squirrel once; that was bad enough. It kept me awake all night.

Torrential rain meant one of two things. It was either going to be an awesome mud bath at soccer where we could slosh and slide around in the muddy puddles, competing to see who could get the dirtiest, or it would be cancelled. I hoped it wouldn't be cancelled. Muddy soccer games were my favorite.

I looked at my Thomas the tank engine clock. It was 8 am. I was supposed to be playing soccer at 8.30am. I went to jump out of the bed in a mad panic, but my legs felt like they were going to explode. I have never known pain like it. They were so sore and stiff. The day before, the muscles felt like they were made of iron ore. Now they were feeling like iron ore on fire. I remembered why I didn't like running. It always made me sore the next day. My 'know it all' mom always said, if I did more exercise more regularly, the muscles would get used to it, and I wouldn't be so sore.

I stumbled out into the lounge room, walking like a grandpa. All I needed was a wheelie walker to lean on and I would be fine. I had a laugh to myself as I imagined hobbling out on an awesome wheelie walker, complete with iPad, snacks, phone; everything a boy could want.

Mom was in the kitchen packing food into boxes and hampers. I didn't really question what she was doing as I was too worried about soccer.

"Mom! Why didn't you wake me up? Where are we playing? How long will it take to get there? I'm hungry." Mom just kept calmly taking food out of the fridge.

"Which one of those questions would you like me to answer first?" she said smugly.

"MOM!"

"RYAN!"

"What?"

"Nothing. I'm just yelling at you like you yelled at me," she stated plainly.

"Oh! Well are we going to soccer?"

"Ryan, look outside. What do you see?"

"Ah, grass, trees, Dad's shed. Mom, I don't want to play eye spy thanks anyway."

"What about the torrential weather out there? It's raining cats and dogs."

"WHERE ARE ALL THE CATS AND DOGS? I don't see any cats and dogs because you and Dad won't let us get one. Are you serious? Soccer's been cancelled again hasn't it?"

"Afraid so," she said with a sympathetic smile, as if she knew how I felt.

"Nooooooo!"

"Yeeeeeees!"

"That's the second time this month."

"Well unfortunately that's what happens with weekend sports sometimes. That's just the way it is. It would be too dangerous playing out on those fields. Anyway, don't forget, Dad is bringing home a super surprise for us at lunchtime; one the whole family will enjoy."

'I've heard that before,' I thought to myself. "Any clues Mom?"

"You'll find out soon enough."

"Oh yeah, can we go and get Matthew a birthday present this morning?"

"Not today darling. I don't have enough time."

"Not today! His party's today. I'm not going to turn up to the party empty handed. I know we should have got it earlier, but I forgot, because I was mentally and physically exhausted with all the running we've had to do at school."

"Well Rino, you said nothing about Matthew's party to me."

"Yeah I did, the other day. Oh no, that was Dad. I told him Matthew's party was on, and he said no worries."

"Ryan, you know Dad never listens to anything, and he always agrees to everything."

"Yeah I know. Anyway, what's the big deal? I'm letting you know now. It's tonight and it's not like we ever go out or anything."

"Well, actually, today we do have plans."

"Plans? What plans? We never have plans. Actually, correction, we only have plans when I already have better plans."

"Ryan, you're not making sense."

"Well Matthew already thinks I'm going. It would be rude not to turn up, and you've always told me it's very rude to be rude." I was starting to get hysterical. This was going to be the most awesome birthday party of the year, and once again, Mom was ruining it.

"Actually, I spoke to Matthew's mother at the market during the week and I told her you couldn't be there. So she understands."

"I don't care if *she* understands. It's not *her* birthday. It's Matthew's birthday, and he won't understand." I could feel tears bubbling in the back of my eye sockets. I tried to breathe controllably and get a grip on myself. I hated crying, but the stinking tears began to escape like waterfalls cascading down a rocky mountain. The salty taste crept into my mouth and reminded me of eating crisps.

I started to run away into my room, but my legs wouldn't move. The agony was unbearable, and the emotional pain inflicted on me by my mother was torture. Everything about the day was terrible. It was the worst day in my whole life, and it was all my mom and dad's fault.

"Ryan, get a grip on yourself." Here she goes again. "You're far too old to be sooking over things like not getting your own way."

"But I **never** get my own way. I never get to do anything good. It's so unfair." I started to shout at my mom, but I realized I would be saying good bye to my Xbox if I yelled at her.

I walked back to my room slowly like an old man. Why does my mom do this to me? Her siri voice in her head must have gone, "DING! Something good is happening for Ryan tonight. Better put some plans into action to annihilate *his* plans."

No soccer

No party

Pouring rain

Dead legs. Life couldn't get much worse………or could it?

14. The Most Embarrassing, Gigantic, Outrageous Monster Ever

After I angrily jumped up and down on my bed, forgetting about my sore legs and breaking the slats, I lay down under the blankets and listened to the cats and dogs (and elephants) pelting on our roof top. I began playing Minecraft to try and numb the pain, and forget how bad my life was at that moment. Mom stormed in at 10am, and told me to close it down and to pack some clothes.

"Really?" I said excitedly. "Can I go to Matthew's party now?" I wanted to run over and hug her but my legs wouldn't move, plus it's kind of uncool hugging your Mom.

"No Ryan," she laughed, "you are not going to Matthew's party. Nothing will change that." She looked out the window as she spoke. "Well, not unless this downpour of rain turns into a cyclone category 3 or a blizzard and we're snowed in. Dad has made plans, and knowing Dad, we will be going even if there *is* a blizzard. He'll find a way, if it means we all have to shovel our way out."

She was right. When my Dad got an idea in his head, NOTHING stopped him. He *would* have us all out in the blizzard shifting snow if it meant carrying on with one of his hair brained ideas. *And* he would think it was family FUN.

"Now start packing! And maybe bring your rain coat......... and your rain boots, and a scarf, just in case it's freezing, and hurry. And NO electronics, I repeat NO elec..."

"I HEARD YOU!" I interrupted. This was just going to be awesome. NOT! NOT! DOUBLE NOT!! Not only was I going to be dragged off to some boring place with my boring family, I wasn't even allowed to take anything remotely fun. 'Well we'll see about that,' I thought to myself, as I grabbed my bag and sneakily shoved my Nintendo DS disguised in a toilet bag inside. I couldn't find the charger so I made a mental note to grab it before we left.

I sulkily packed a few things into the bag. I had no idea where we were going or for how long. All I knew was, it was going to be boring and miserable with horrible weather. Hopefully I would be able to spend some time rugged up in the car playing my DS.

To add to my excitement, Lisa came bursting in, full of unrestrained enthusiasm, giggling all over the place.

"I can't wait until Dad gets home with the surprise can you?"

"Ah der, yeah, I *can* wait. I'm happy to wait another century actually."

"It's going to be so awesome I can't wait. I'm so glad I haven't got anything on this weekend. I would hate to miss out on the surprise. I wonder what it is going to be. Mom's asked us to pack clothes. I wonder if we might be going to some 5 star tropical resort somewhere with gorgeous surfers. Do you think I should take my bikini? Ryan? RYAN ARE YOU LISTENING TO ME?"

I tune out when all I can hear is blah, blah blahdey blah.

"Yep whatever ya reckon," I answered.

"What, I should take my bikinis? You think it's going to be somewhere hot? Do you think we'll go on a plane?"

The last thing I wanted to think about in my misery, was my sister's bikinis. I couldn't care less whether she took a couple of garbage bags with arms holes, and a paper bag for a hat. Actually maybe she would look better with a paper bag over her head, with 2 holes for her eyes.

"Ryan! I'm talking to you!"

"I know. That's the problem. If you stop talking to me, then we have no problem. YES! Take your bikinis. We are probably going to Hawaii, and on the way we'll do a lap around Bali, then off to Phuket, so take your bikinis, take ten pairs of bikinis for all I care."

"I think you're lying."

I didn't answer.

"Ryan, are you lying? Don't get me excited for no reason please." Oh wow, I didn't know how dumb my sister really was. Maybe I needed to be a bit nicer to her. I didn't know she had such a serious problem with her intelligence levels.

"I'm just kidding Lisa. I really need to concentrate on what I'm packing, so if you don't mind."

"Ok, well I guess if Mom wants us to pack stuff, then the surprise probably isn't going to be a puppy?" Oh Wow. She was so clued up that girl.

"Yes Lisa. I think you're right there." She left disappointed that I didn't share her girlie enthusiasm in Mom and Dad's little family surprises. Lisa was older than me, but I was way more mature that's for sure.

Dad usually finished work on a Saturday morning at 12 noon. At 12.23p.m. precisely, Lisa started screaming, "Dad's home, Dad's home. I

71

heard him toot in the driveway." She came screeching into my room again (she will never learn). "Quick Rino, come out with me. Let's greet him together." WOW! That would be so cool. NOT! Her and I skipping down the driveway together to greet our daddy. That moment wasn't going to happen in a hurry.

Lisa did a skip and clapped her legs in the air as she ran out. I went over to my window to see if it was Dad, and to look for clues. I opened the blinds, and through the drizzle I saw it. Dad kept tooting to announce his arrival. 'Holy rootin tootin titanic', was all I could say to myself. It was GIGANTIC! Actually gigantic is not the word. It was so big, it made the Titanic look like a baby's tug boat toy.

15. My Worst Nightmare

"AGHHHHHHHH!" I flung myself back on my bed. Why was this happening to me? What did I ever do to deserve this suffering? I must have been a crazed armed robber in a previous life to have this continuous suffering inflicted on my poor youthful soul.

I had spent the past week praying to God that the surprise would be something cool like an updated Xbox or a new Nintendo, or iPad or something like that. Even a puppy would have been awesome, but no, Dad had to bring home this…..this …monstrosity. Did he actually expect us to get in it? Did he actually expect that we would be seen in public in it? Did he actually think it would make it to the end of the street? There was only one thing I could do now.

Pray again. For a cyclone category 5.

"Rino, come on down, your father has something to show you," Mom sang. She always spoke in a sing song voice when she was all cheery about something. I wished I could turn myself into a Minecraft Enderman and teleport myself right out of the house and down the street to Matthew's house without anyone knowing I had gone.

It was too late. My mom walked into my bedroom carrying something in a bag. It looked like clothing.

"Come on honey bun." I hated it when she called me that. It made me feel like I was ten months old, not ten years. "I have something special for you to wear. It's cold outside so I want you to wear this when we go down to see Dad's surprise. It's a surprise for Dad, to thank him for his surprise."

73

I pushed the edges out of the corner of my mouth and tried to fake a smile. Though my stomach was twisted into a knotted mess and my heart was tormented inside, I didn't want to let Mum know. I hated to disappoint her when they had obviously gone to so much trouble, so I pretended to be excited, though I don't think I would have won any academy awards for my acting.

"Sure Mom, what is it?" If we were going out in the wild weather in that thing, I would be happy to wear any warm clothing Mom gave me, so I took the parcel from her.

"Hurry and put it on, and quickly come downstairs. Lisa's waiting. Where's your bag?" She grabbed the bag and dashed off as quickly as she came.

I opened the bag and pulled out a thick, woolly, blue sweater. It was my favorite color. As I went to pull it over my head, I gasped in horror when I saw the print on the front. It was my worst nightmare. It was more terrifying than the thing out the front. I was caught smack bang in the middle of my worst nightmare. I wanted to go back to sleep and dream of Zombie Pigmen trying to attack me with axes disguised as birthday presents or some other Minecraft madness.

Anything would be better than the horrifying nightmare that was my reality. I pinched myself to make sure it was real. "Ow!" I said when I squeezed too tightly. There was some horror movie in the olden days called 'Nightmare on Elm St'. I felt like I was trapped in 'a Nightmare on Elm St meets 'Diary of a wimpy kid: the Long Haul.'

16. The Wimpy Kid's Limo Ride to Disaster

I slowly walked down the stairs in my treasured sweater. And there, horror upon horror, was Lisa and Mom standing in matching sweaters. Lisa's was pink of course  because everything Lisa owns is pink. Mom's was pale blue and I could see she was carrying one the same as mine for Dad. Mom's face was gleaming, she was so proud. It looked like she knitted them herself. "Let's go see Dad," she said excitedly, and we all walked out with our matching sweaters displaying a big family portrait on the front of each one, with the words 'The James mob' on the back.

Our faces looked like mugshots taken from a high security jail. My mouth looked like it was as big as my whole face and Lisa looked like Mrs. Potato head. Mom looked ok because her face was blurry and Dad's head resembled a tiny pimple on a big body because he was going bald. The photo was in one word, UGLY.

Much to my horror, I could now see, as I had my mental breakdown inside, that the same mugshot graced the sides of the monstrous vehicle that loomed menacingly in our driveway, inviting nervous stares from the neighbors.

Lisa's mouth dropped open and hit the ground. I had to pick it up for her and scrape the gravel off before the flies got inside. I guessed that she was just as shocked as I was, at the prospect of getting in that thing.

Dad tooted again and waved at us with a big toothy grin from way up high in the driver's seat of the oldest, weirdest looking bus I had ever seen. It was painted a bright blue and had brightly painted yellow flowers along the sides and our faces were plastered on the side in the same family portrait. This time the caption on the bus said, '*The James family have gone campin'*. What did that even mean?

I was horrified. I wanted to melt into the ground and be sucked away into the abyss, never to be found. I'm sure my family would miss me....for a day, maybe even two, but they'd get over it by having so much fun on their busovan camping trip. I couldn't possibly drive through the town with my oversized mouth plastered all over the bus. I knew too many people. I would be history. I would be known as Rino the bus boy. Or worse, Rino the flower bus boy.

But all through my anguish, I squeezed out the biggest, fakest smile that I could muster. Amongst all the distress I felt inside, it kinda felt good to see my Mom and Dad so proud and blissfully happy.

Some of the kids at school only had one parent, which was fine, but it was nice to know that I had two parents who wanted to make us stick together and have fun as a family, even if I did still feel like screaming. "AGGGGGGGGGGHHHHHHHHHHHHHHHHHH!" There! I let it out, internally, and it felt great. It felt really great. But just to be sure, I screamed louder inside my head, where my thoughts and my hysterical screams were private, and no-one could hear me going quietly psycho. **"EEEEEEEEEEEEE!"** **"AAAGGHHHHHHH!"**

Feeling slightly better, I waved at Dad and climbed aboard, turning round to smile at Mom who was beaming brighter than a rainbow. Lisa, on the other hand was looking stunned, and was not doing anything to hide her disappointment. I'm not sure what she was hoping for, but it obviously wasn't a bus van thingy, whatever Dad wanted to call it. I think she would have preferred the pet ant actually; even a green one.

I stepped aboard and immediately a bit of metal from the step fell to the ground. Great! Not only was this the most embarrassing bus ever, it was probably the most dangerous bus ever.

"Ahh she'll be right Rino, just pick it up and jump aboard," Dad said. I had a thought that I was desperately going to need some comfort food to save me from this trip, and knowing my mom, she wouldn't have packed anything junky, so I told Dad I needed to go and pee, and quickly went back inside before Mom locked up.

I ran to her secret stash that she keeps in her sock draw to see if I could find anything yummy, but to my despair, there was nothing there. The cupboard was bare....again. Thanks Mrs. Hubbard for nothing. Maybe Mom had packed some stuff already. But I would have to wait for her scummy rations once a day probably.

"All aboard," Dad called out. Lisa was still standing like a stunned mullet in the same position with her chin starting to drop to the ground again. I could definitely see a swarm of blow flies hanging around ready to start a party inside.

"I'm NOT getting in that thing," she said. "I'll split my shorts."

"Well you shouldn't wear them so tight," I said. Lisa could be so selfish sometimes. Couldn't she see that 'thing' was making Mom and Dad very happy?

Dad tooted and cranked up the engine. It kicked over loudly, gurgled and spluttered before cutting out. Oh dear!

"Not a problem," Dad said. "It just needs a bit of turbo boost." He flicked the switch again and the engine roared into action like a dragon spitting fire.

"Move it or lose it," I called out from the step to Lisa.

"Oh you be quiet, you useless fart bucket." Of course she said that one under her breath so Mom and Dad, both inside the bus, couldn't hear. My lovely sister! A whole weekend away with her, jammed up inside a bus playing scrabble. At least I would have my Nintendo DS, I thought, as Dad putted down the street.

'Oh no!' I thought, when I realized I'd forgotten to put the charger in. Horror washed over me in waves of despair. No junk food. No Nintendo, and Lisa for the whole weekend in a broken down bus with flowers and our mug shots on the side. This road trip was going to make The Wimpy Kid's 'Long Haul' look like a limo ride to Disneyland.

17. So Where do we Pee and Poop?

I had a quick look around the bus before Dad told me to belt up (meaning put the seatbelt on…..I think). I actually couldn't believe my eyes! Inside the bus, it was kind of awesome really. It was like a mini motel on wheels. It had a fridge, a microwave, cupboards and beds!! We were going to *sleep* on the bus! And the best part about it, was that the single beds *weren't* together.

I looked inside the fridge and there was heaps of yummy food in there. There was even a tap with running water. Not sure how that was going to work. It was like a mini house on wheels, but there was one thing missing.

"Hey Dad, so um, like where do we pee and poop?"

"In the bush," he replied.

Hook line and sinker, in she came as expected.

"I WILL NOT PEE IN A BUSH!" Lisa shrieked. "I will twist my legs around themselves for the whole weekend if I have to, but I am not doing anything in the bush unless it involves binoculars and a nature trail." Lisa always bites at Dad's jokes. At least, I hoped he was just joking.

After what seemed like an eternity of bumpy travelling along gravelly roads, Dad pulled into a gas station in the middle of a country town. It looked like a scene from an old country and western movie with dusty red roads framed by scraggly bushes and tumbleweed blowing down the deserted street. We'd definitely left the rain behind. I must have been sleeping, because the last thing I remember was kicking back in the reclining chair, turning on this awesome radio built into the wall, closing,

then opening my eyes, to find that my
body had turned kind of all blocky.
Everything about me looked like
rectangular bricks.

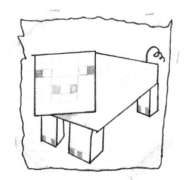

As I looked at my strangely
shaped body, I found myself marching
through barren grass with trees and
bushes around me that looked like blocks. I hadn't walked very far when
I came across this cute little pig.

I was just about to pick up the pig when a pack of untamed
wolves jumped down in front of me, eyeing off the pig hungrily and
looking at me with venom. Now normally, if I was confronted by such a
frightening scenario, I would start shaking in my boots and scream
"MOMMYYYYYYY!" But for some unknown reason, this wave of
bravado overcame me and I gallantly drew a sword, (that I didn't even
know I had) from my belt and slashed at the angry wolves. "I will save
you oh piglet," I said in a voice fit for a dashing prince. Their eyes bulged
red, piercing right through me. Then, surprisingly, I found a bone in my
back pocket.

Waving the bone in their faces, the wolves mellowed and I was
able to befriend the beasts, so we all marched merrily through a jungle
together, fighting off evil creatures in search of treasure.

I had only just come to a medieval castle when I heard a loud
engine sound rumbling in the distance. As the sound grew louder, it

 became clear to me that it was the raucous rumble of
the flower bus stalling its engine as we rolled into a

gas station. I guessed I'd been having another one of my mad Minecraft dreams again.

We all got off the bus and left Dad to fill up the tank. I estimated it would probably take half the day to fill that thing so Mom and Lisa went into the shop, and I went exploring round the back looking for the bathroom. What I found looked more like a bucket with a lid on it and a piece of timber hanging off an old, weathered frame for a door. I debated whether I should just hold on and wait for the next roadside stop, and hope it had at least a one star rating, because this place definitely had no stars. If there was such a thing as a negative star review, this gas station would be about a negative 2 star rating

I opened the toilet lid and just as quickly slammed it down again wanting to gag. Words cannot begin to describe my horror and fright. I ran out traumatized screaming, "AGGGGGGGGGGGGGGGHHHHHH!"

From that moment on, I knew I would need a life of post traumatic counselling and psychotherapy to help me move beyond the experience. I grabbed Lisa as she came out of the shop, and pulled her towards the bus.

"Let's get out of here quick," I stuttered, still traumatized.

"What? Let go! What are you dragging me for? Mom! Ryan's gone insane…again."

"Can we just go? This place is YUK!"

"I just want to go to the bathroom first," she said, pulling away from my grip.

"Noooooo!" I shouted, suddenly protective of my sister.

"You are so mad. I need to go to the bathroom," she said taking out her lip-gloss. As if the twenty layers she'd already put on that day weren't enough already.

"Lisa, don't! You'll regret it. There's a ...." I couldn't even say it.

"There's a what?"

"There's a ....there's a gigantic poo floating round the top, sticking out. It was literally staring at me bobbing in the murky water. I've never seen anything like it."

"Eewgh! YOU ARE SO GROSS! I'm going to use the ladies bathroom inside. You should have used the men's inside. It was probably you anyway and now you're trying to blame someone else because you can't flush it. Eewgh, you're such a nerd turd."

The sound of the word 'turd' sent a nauseating wave through my stomach. I ran behind the bus and dry wretched. Nothing came out, but I felt better even though I was still busting to do a pee. I climbed aboard the bus and jumped back into the recliner and hoped the next stop wasn't too far away. I closed my eyes and wished myself back into my land of Minecraft madness where fighting evil zombies was far less scarier than what I'd just experienced.

18. One Million Things I'd Rather be Doing

Dad had bought a hotdog from the gas station. I think it was one of those microwave ones. I'd seen more hotdog than I needed to at that gas station, so I chose to opt for one of Mom's peanut butter sandwiches. She was quite taken aback when I said I didn't want any junk food.

"Are you coming down with a fever?" she asked.

"Of course he is. It's a bad case of weirdo fever. I've told you that before Mom," Lisa piped in.

"Lisa, enough. There's no need for that. Can we just have one weekend without any bickering?" I think my Mom says that every weekend. Probably every day actually. But she was right. Lisa and I were always squabbling and 'hanging it' on each other. I decided I would try and make an effort to get along with her over the weekend, even if all she talked about was clothes and makeup. Beats fighting all the time.

I was trying to get back to Minecraft dreamland again but my drowsiness was hacked with the terrible sounds of screeching. I thought Dad was having a heart attack, until I looked up and saw him jigging around in the driver's seat, singing at the top of his very unmusical voice. He was using the hotdog as a microphone, *and* eating it very grossly at the same time, with sauce dripping out of the corners of his mouth.

Finally, the dismal reality of Dad singing love songs to his hotdog, Lisa looking at herself in the mirror and Mom snoring her head off, were blocked out, and I fell into a land where nothing else was important except

building cities, fighting zombies and searching for treasure.

I'm not sure how long I might have been asleep, but I woke up again abruptly when the old flower bus roared over a big bump, and crash landed into a puddle creating an awesome stream of white wash up the sides. As it landed, I head butted the sides of the window. I'm sure the bus became airborne for a split second and I thought I might have to change the name to 'The Flying Flower bus'.

"Cool Dad. That was cool. Can we hit the decks like that again?"

"NO! We can not do that again," Mom said sternly, giving Dad one of those looks that meant *don't you dare do that again*. Dad actually looked quite pale and he was gripping on to the steering wheel like he was superglued to it. Mom then began speaking to him in that tone that always got him shaking in his boots. Maybe he didn't mean to do a Monster bus action stunt show on purpose. Whoops!

I looked out the window to see that the rain had returned lightly. All this rain, and I still hadn't seen one cat or dog.

"Are we there yet Dad?" Lisa whined. I don't know how many times she'd asked him that. It reminded me of the ad on TV when the kid keeps asking his Dad like over and over, "are we there yet Dad?" Lisa is so good at being a pain; a pain in the butt cheeks.

"Not yet princess." Ewgh! Aren't princesses supposed to be beautiful, sweet and loving? Yeah right! Like that's Lisa all over. NOT!!! Although most of the time Lisa thinks of herself as a princess. It's a wonder she doesn't wear a tiara around the place.

"How long Dad?"

"About an hour buddy. Hold on tight. We'll be there soon."

"How long are we going for?" I'd only just realized that I didn't know where, or for how long we were going.

"Just a couple of nights. You're gonna have a ball."

Yeah right! I could think of a million things I'd rather be doing than spending a wet, miserable weekend stuck in a bus covered in flowers playing scrabble with my sister. Like:

1. Scrubbing the toilets in every public amenity block,

2. Picking up dog poo at the royal dog show,

3. Squeezing Lisa's zits for her. Her nickname is Zittany Spears,

4. Having to do homework with Nasty Nige. Actually that wouldn't be too bad.

5. GOING TO MATTHEW'S BIRTHDAY PARTY!!!!!!!

I decided to try and take my mind off things for the last hour and use up my remaining battery power in the Nintendo DS. I rumbled in my back pack and grabbed 'How to train your Dragon' and stared at the cover for a while. I tried to turn on the Nintendo but it wouldn't power on. I pushed the button again and again getting more frustrated with each push. If I was allowed to swear I would have popped one out right then. Instead I just let a few go inside my head. IT WAS FLAT!

IT WAS F. L. A. T. FLAT!

AGHHHHHHHHHH! (again)

I couldn't believe it. My last twenty minutes of happiness and it had been cruelly taken away from me. I thought back to Wednesday night when I'd gone to bed and couldn't sleep. I'd snuck out of my bed to get my Nintendo and played it under the covers until I drifted off to sleep. In the morning my Nintendo was sleeping too, and I'd never gotten round to charging it. AGHHHHHH!

I sat back in my seat and waited until we arrived, trying to contain my excitement, which wasn't really hard as I didn't have any. Lisa kept whinging for the last half hour, wanting to know every five minutes how long to go. In the end Dad just said, "Five minutes less than last time you asked."

Lisa ended up cracking it and keeping quiet. Finally she drifted off to sleep and I looked up towards God and thanked him quietly. But it wasn't long before Dad slowed the bus down, (although I didn't think it could go much slower) and shouted, "we're here!" Then he started singing again, some crazy made up song.

"We're here, we're here,
we're really, really here.
Let's sing, let's dance.
I think I need a beer,"

and he laughed at himself hysterically, while Mom rolled her eyes.

I looked out of the bus to see an enormous entrance gate enclosing a forest like parkland with rich, green trees lining the driveway. As we entered through the massive gates, I could see a crystal clear dam with boats and canoes bobbing merrily up and down on its surface. Some other floating bike like machines with inflated wheels rested on the water's edge. On the other side I saw a flying fox that seemed to stretch forever.

"Cooooooooool," was all I could say.

"Awesome," Lisa added, as she came out of her beauty sleep twenty hours too early.

We drove slowly through, reveling in each new discovery as we ventured further into the park. There were playgrounds, water slides, tennis courts, rope climbing courses, and the best thing by far was a go cart track. I couldn't see any go-carts, so I hoped they were stored somewhere and you didn't have to bring your own. The only time I ever had a go kart was when Dad made me one when I was eight. It was awesome, until I got in it and tried to ride it. The wheels fell off, shortly followed by the steering wheel. So we never ventured down that path again.

The place looked awesome. It probably even had a games room somewhere. Imagine that! A games room with an XBOX 1, Wii and PlayStation4. That would be like camping heaven.

If only the rain could stop! I decided, even if it continued to fall, I was still going to get out and have a go at everything, even if I had to get out in my embarrassing canary colored rain jacket with matching rain boots. Ugly as they were, they were better than my Thomas the tank coat which was two sizes too small, with matching Percy and Gordon boots.

After Dad checked in at the office, he followed the map he was given and turned down this little lane way. I had no idea how he was going to turn the corner or make the bus fit down the street.

"Breathe in," he said to everybody, as we putted down the lane. I actually saw Lisa breathe in deeply. Gosh she could be easy to fool sometimes. I saw Mom breathe in too, but I think she was holding her breath, out of fear that we were going to collect a few tree branches on our way. I hoped Dad had a license for the flower bus. There were a few moments when I wasn't too convinced.

A peaceful river meandered along the side of the lane way, with mini waterfalls trickling over rocky bulges. "Wow. Did you bring the boogie board Dad?" I could just picture myself cascading down the waterfalls. "Can we go swimming in the river?"

"Not on your Nellie," came the sharp reply. Who was Nellie? "Don't you even think about it, especially with this rain. You never know what eddies are underneath."

"Who is Eddie?" I asked, wondering who all these people were that he was talking about.

"Oh you're such a dork Ryan. He means Eddie Krueger from those horror movies, 'Nightmare on Elm St' don't you Dad?" Lisa answered conceitedly.

"No, I mean eddies and currents that can be lurking under a peaceful surface and can take you downstream or suck you under. An eddy is a swirling of water in the opposite direction to the current. Just stay away from the river."

We finally managed to crawl into a camping site. Fortunately, it was big enough to take the bus, even if Dad did have to do a ten point turn to get in. There was a little old caravan about the size of a match box car parked next to our site. It looked like it was as ancient as our bus. We had neighbors! This could be a good thing or a bad thing.

I glanced out of the windows to see if I could see some kids hanging around. That would make the whole weekend a lot more bearable. But all I could see was a little old man with wiry hair and Harry Potter glasses sitting in a camp chair, reading a book. Wow! He looked like he was going to be a real blast. Then I saw something exciting next to him, and I knew then, that it didn't matter how bad or how rainy this weekend was, I was going to have a great time.

19. Dog Days and Flying Foxes

I bounded out of the bus faster than a supersonic robot doing the zombie Olympics and went over to the old man.

When I approached, I realized he wasn't reading a book, he was sleeping with his book over his face. Little tails started wagging from the basket sitting at his feet. If I had a tail, it would have started wagging as well, I was so excited. If there's one thing I love more than PlayStation and Minecraft, it's the XBOX1. No, only joking. It's dogs. I love dogs. I'm obsessed with dogs. I really do love them more than..........well maybe not quite. Ever since our dog Pugsley was ravaged by green ants and died a few years ago, I've been desperate for a new one. So has Lisa. It's the only thing we agree on.

I've even told Mom and Dad that my PlayStation obsession is probably pent up madness about not having a dog. If I had a dog I wouldn't need to be playing computer games all the time. Well that's what I tell them anyway. Secretly I have these little images of sitting in the bean bag with my puppy on my lap and my remote control in my hands. Then when I get really carried away dreaming, I have visions of me in one bean bag versing the dog in the other bean bag as we go head to head in combat in Dragon Ball Z.

The little dogs started to creep out of their basket timidly. They were so cute cuddled up together but they obviously were cautious about the old man allowing them to move away.

"Hey boy," I said to the larger one. He looked like a cattle dog, and I couldn't wait to ask if I could walk him.

"It's a girl," said the old man waking up. I hoped he was a nice old man and not one of those grumpy types you hear about.

"Can I pat her?"

"Sure, but she'll probably follow you around for life then."

"That's cool," I said, stroking the dog as she eagerly lapped it up. The little white fluffy one got jealous and started edging her snout under my hand.

"Oh my God!" Lisa had found out my secret and bounded out of the bus. "Mom! It's a white fluffy handbag dog." I felt so sorry for the old man. He was probably thinking his peaceful camping holiday had just been trashed by a zombie doll in pink lip gloss.

"Oh can I hold her please?" Lisa asked, referring to the white fluffy thing.

"Yes you may young lady, but she's a he."

"And don't go putting it in your hand bag," I said under my breath, as I started throwing a ball to the big dog. Tess was her name. Lisa started making these goo goo gaga noises at the dog like it was a baby in a blanket.

Mom and Dad came over and introduced themselves *and* apologized for their overeager, rude children. They really hit it off, and Mom and Dad spent a lot of the day talking with the old fella. Dad even went fishing with him when the rain eased, which was cool with me because I haven't developed my Dad's love for fishing yet. I have this problem about wasting hours on end standing on the edge of a river bank waiting for a fish that never comes. So at least Bob (the old man) stopped Dad from bugging me about going.

Lisa and I hung out together for the rest of the day doing all the activities including the go-karts. The rain came in patches but didn't dampen our spirits, even if it did dampen our clothes. The flying fox was awesome. Part of it went over a mini lake and you could fly off and crash land making thunder splashes.

The air had a biting chill to it when I was wet, but it wasn't cold enough for Lisa not to wear her bikini. She thinks she looks so good in it, she probably would wear it in a blizzard.

I had a major laughing attack when Lisa did a big spill off the flying fox. She crash landed into the water so fast, her bikini top flew off. When she came out of the water, she didn't realize until a little girl started pointing at her and laughing.

"Look Mommy, boobies," she'd said to her mother who was also laughing, I think. There weren't many people around because it was chilly, so no-one really saw her, but her face was a color any tomato would be proud of. I just couldn't stop laughing, I nearly peed myself.

"Stop it!" Lisa said with a cranky face, as she tried to tie the bows up again. "It's not funny!"

"Correction. It's hilarious," I replied between gasps of uncontrollable laughter. Boy I could be a mean brother. Serves her right for all the mean things she'd done to me in the past.

She finally forgot about her fashion parade disaster and then we went onto the adventure playground where we rock climbed, abseiled and climbed all these ropes. Once again Lisa proved to be a real dare devil, and I forgot momentarily that she was my sister, and we just hung out and competed against each other in everything.

I was devastated when she beat me on the ropes course. Actually I was mortified, and so embarrassed. Being beaten by a girl in a bikini. Worse still, that girl was my sister!

And some six year old boys saw us, and they started chanting, "beaten by a girl, beaten by a girl," as they giggled, thinking they were so cool. If only they knew how uncool they really looked. I'm sure I was never that uncool when I was that age.

Luck was on our side and the rain that threatened ominously all day stayed away and was replaced by light showers that cooled us. We ran from activity to activity, and in between, I went back to throw the ball to Tess, who got excited every time she saw me approaching. Her wagging tail became like a violent weapon the closer I got to her. Her teeth shone brightly and her tongue panted, with dog saliva dripping to the ground. That's the only thing I don't like about dogs, when they drool. That, and their poo.

She looked like she was smiling. In fact, I think she *was* smiling and so was I; from ear to ear and all the way round my head. I was doing a 360 degree smile. I don't even think playing a PlayStation game could make me do a 360 smile. Come to think of it, when I won the PlayStation 4 at Movie World, my smile did do a 360, and it probably ran laps around my face, I couldn't stop grinning.

But this was a different kind of happiness; a different kind of awesomeness. It's really hard to explain how good it was to have a little mate to run around with all the time, and to care for, and talk to when everyone else was driving me mad.

I asked Bob if I could feed them that night. He seemed very pleased. He said he would be very happy to let his rickety old legs stay in the chair for a bit longer. He definitely wasn't a grumpy old man, and he kept giving Lisa and I candy all the time much to Mom's disgust, though I saw her taking a couple when she didn't think we were looking. Mom's the candy fairy; she buys candy, hides it, and then does this magic trick where in the morning it's disappeared.

Before supper, Dad suggested that we all go for a walk up to see the waterfalls, before it started raining heavily again, as the clouds were starting to loom. Lisa had her usual whine when anyone mentioned the word 'walk' but Dad assured us we wouldn't have to go far. We were both exhausted.

I asked Bob if I could take Tess and Max with us, but Dad, who always likes to poop on a party because he's a party pooper, said no, we had to protect the wildlife.

"Well *they* could protect *us* from the wildlife," I said to Dad pleading with him. He looked around at their angelic faces that wouldn't hurt a fly and just laughed at me.

"The answer's no, bud. Don't bring it up again. Get your rain jacket."

Disappointed, I raced off to get ready for the bush walk. Dad asked Bob if he wanted to come but he said he was going inside to have a nap before supper.

Mom asked Bob if he would like to come over to ours for supper and he cordially accepted the invitation. Sounded a bit strange saying to someone, "would you like to come over to our bus for supper?"

Mom got some of the food out of the fridge while we were putting on our rain gear. She started setting up a little picnic on the table in front of the annex. I'm not sure what was in the picnic basket but it smelt delicious. I couldn't wait to eat. After all the action of the day, I was starved. I could have eaten ten hamburgers, maybe twenty at a push. I could only imagine what it must be like to be a superhero; leaping tall buildings, zooming through the sky propelled by supersonic forces, catapulting out of skyscrapers and saving little fat ladies and their puppies. They must eat for days just to get enough energy.

Just as we started our walk, Lisa had to run back to the camp site for some annoying reason. She said she wanted to grab her backpack.

"Why do you need your backpack to go walking?" I called out. She probably wanted to take her lip gloss, eyeshadow, mirror, mascara, blusher and whatever the other gunk is that girls paint on their faces. She ignored me and Dad told her to catch up to us.

"We haven't got time to be hanging around waiting. I think there's going to be a storm," Dad said. There was a distant rumble of thunder as Dad spoke, and the sky was looking pretty gloomy. I can remember when I was little, I used to get really frightened of thunder. As I clung to Mom's legs with snot dripping out of my nose, bawling my eyes out, she would tell me it was Santa Claus packing all the toys in boxes getting ready for Christmas. As if!

Sadly, I used to believe her until third grade when our science teacher told us thunder was 'the expansion of rapidly heated air because of the sudden increase in pressure and temperature after a lightning strike. It creates a sonic shock wave, similar to a sonic boom which produces the sound of thunder'. After that, I was absolutely crushed. All those years of thinking I was hearing Santa packing his boxes. I then became paranoid and hysterical again every time I heard thunder and lightning. In case you hadn't realized, I led a tortured childhood.

Half way through the walk, I kept hallucinating that I was hearing the dogs yap. I thought I must have been so keen to get back and play with them that my mind was playing tricks on me. Lisa was acting really weird the whole walk. She kept lagging behind and stopping all the time.

I didn't blame her because Dad kept being all scientific and trying to tell us the names of different plant species using their scientific name. I think he was mostly making them up, because no-one could remember all that stuff unless you were a freaky science professor crossed with a wizard. Maybe Mr. Higginbottom would know that stuff though because he was so smart. I really wished he was going to be at school so I could tell him all about the weekend.

I decided I was getting a bit bored with Dad's impromptu botany lessons, so I thought I might annoy Lisa and start chasing her and maybe do a bit of Kung Fu sparring and tackle her to the ground. I turned off the path and ran screeching down towards her. She panicked in a very unusual way. She almost looked terrified.

"Stay away you crazy zombie madman. Ryan, I'm warning you, back off," she pleaded as I started karate kicking the air around her, laughing. "Ryan please, I'm begging you," she whispered under her breath. That was odd. Usually by that stage she's screaming uncontrollably. She kept dancing on the spot trying to back away.

"Come on you kids. Stop that nonsense," called out Dad.

I expected Lisa to respond with her normal tattle tale whiny voice and call out to Mom, "MOOOOOOOOOOOOM. Ryan's attacking me. Save me!" but she kept silent. She just kept dancing around on her toes looking ridiculous trying to protect her backpack. She looked very odd. And then I saw why she was behaving strangely; more strange than normal.

"You naughty girl," I said laughing. "SPRUNG BAD!"

20. Dog Napper

I looked guiltily around at Mom and Dad to see what they were doing, as the little fluffy white head popped out of Lisa's back pack.

"Does Bob know, or did you dog nap him?"

"Well, he was asleep."

"Oh, you are in so much trouble. You're a dog napper," I said trying to rev her up.

"He was lonely. He wanted to come. It's no fun for him sitting in a basket all day."

"What if Bob wakes up and he sees the dog missing? He could panic or something. Or worse, call the police. Let me have a hold and I won't say anything."

"NO! Mom and Dad will see. Oh god they're coming back."

My heart started racing even though it was Lisa who would be in trouble. I wanted to help her keep Max a secret. It would be our little secret. She was so naughty, it was funny.

"I think we'll head back," Dad announced, fast approaching us. Lisa took off quickly, obviously not wanting Dad to get too close.

"What's wrong with you princess? Do I smell or something? I promise I won't fart. Walk with your ol' Dad," he yelled out after her.

"It's ok Dad. She's in one of those weirdo moods, and your botany lessons probably weren't helping either."

"I HEARD THAT," Lisa shouted as she sprinted off down the track, obviously not wanting Max, who was trying to pop his head out, to be seen. I laughed to myself hysterically. Dad gave me a puzzled look.

"Well you're obviously having a good old time."

"I am Dad. I definitely am," I said, surprising myself. But I had to admit that I was having a fantastic time. The only problem was, whenever I have a fantastic time, something disastrous usually happens to ruin it. And this time, it had nothing to do with my family!

21. Nightmare on Zombie Street

As we reached the edge of the van park, the clouds had enclosed around us, and the sky was looking really threatening. Lisa raced ahead at a speed that would make the road runner proud.

"Wants to get in before the rain messes her hair," Dad laughed.

"Yeah Dad, you're probably right," I couldn't help laughing as we ambled along. "And she's probably worried that her mascara will drip in the rain and make her look like Dracula's daughter again." We all laughed. Inwardly, I thought Lisa always resembled Dracula's daughter anyway.

When we finally got back to the camp site, things didn't seem quite right. Lisa was nowhere in sight and there seemed to be bits of rubbish and debris all over the place. I have this weird internal radar inside me that detects 'perilous danger ahead', and it was working overtime. My blood was surging through my veins, creating a hurricane feeling throughout my body. The little gremlin that lives inside me and only comes out during a threatening situation, started to knock on the inside of my throat, until it was full on beating a drum solo. Something was definitely wrong. Birds screeched in the sky above, leaving their trees, when they'd normally be settling for the night. The thunder rolls were fast approaching but an eeriness overshadowed their roars.

The picnic table looked like a cyclone had ripped menacingly through it. At first we thought it was caused by a wind gust, but as we approached, we realized there was something more at large.

"What the....?" Dad said.

"What the ....?" Mom repeated.

"What the ....?" I added, because I was just as flabbergasted as they were.

I'd never seen anything as eerie as the scene that lay before us. The picnic basket had been turned upside down, and the neatly placed napkins and cutlery that Mom had set up were strewn across the ground, and chairs had been upended. Scraps of food were spread from one end of our campsite to the other.

"Wind or ......?" Mom looked at Dad.

"This isn't the work of wind." Dad replied. "This has come from something angrier than wind, hungrier than wind and more frightening than wind," he said quietly, obviously not wanting me to hear, but not doing a very good job.

There was no-one else to be seen around the camping ground. Apart from the few tents and abandoned caravans that dotted the lane, the park looked deserted. Backed by the thunderous rolls and the flashes of lightning advancing quickly, I could have easily believed I was on the set of a horror movie.

"Where's Lisa?" Dad yelled in a panicked voice. "LISA! LISA!" I looked from Mom's worried face to Dad's panic stricken one, and then to the dog's basket where Tess usually lay sleeping. Tess wasn't there, and I had no idea where Max was either. When we found Lisa, we would probably find Max, but were we going to find Lisa? How could she just 'disappear' so quickly? Suddenly my sister became more important to me than I had ever realized. That gremlin that had been lurking in my throat resurfaced, and this time he was savage.

22. Where's Lisa?

Dad ran up the road as the wind started to howl. "Get in the van," he ordered with force.

"Dad it's a bus."

"Just get in!" His tone was really scaring me. I'd never seen Dad in such a panic before. Mom grabbed my arm and dragged me up the steps. The gentle rain grew heavier just as we were boarding. She then ran back outside and frantically gathered up some of the furniture and put it in the annex. "GET IN THE BUS, AND LOCK THE DOOR," I heard Dad scream as he disappeared into the distance.

The trees outside began swirling in the wind and pounding the edge of the bus in a frightening display. At one point I thought I felt the bus sway, but I think it was just the movement of the branches and the rain whirling in gusts that made me delusional.

Mom and I sat huddled in the front seat listening to the damaging storm build up. She kept looking out the window. I'm not sure but I think I might have seen a small tear escaping from the corner of her eye.

"It's ok Mom," I said, not really knowing what to say. It wasn't every day you had to comfort your Mother, and I was kind of out of practice. "We'll be ok."

"It's not us that I'm worried about," she said and she gasped as though she was trying to hold back tears.

I'm not sure how long we were sitting there with Mom holding onto me tightly. I didn't have the heart to tell her that I couldn't breathe, and I was starting to get pins and needles in my fingers where she was cutting off the circulation. It might have been about five or ten minutes. We'd lost sight of the view outside as the windows were fogging up and the sky had become dark and shadowy. All we could hear was the thunderous roars of the storm until finally, Dad's heavy boots could be heard thumping up the steps, opening the bus door quickly. Mom sprang out of the seat and dissolved into tears as soon as she saw Lisa. She flung her arms around her and I was able to breathe again, because:

1. Mom had stopped strangling me and,
2. Lisa was back.

I kind of had this little urge to go and give her a hug, but I quickly pushed it back into the depths of wherever it came from. It definitely wouldn't have been cool. But I was glad she was ok.

"Mom there was a grizzly bear," she spoke quickly, her eyes beaming with excitement, "and everyone said he was angry and on a rampage. So they all took shelter up at the community hall. He must have taken our food because when I got back it was everywhere."

"Where's Max?" I said loudly. I was done with being worried about Lisa. I just wanted to know that she got Max back to safety, and didn't leave him somewhere for the grizzly bear to mistake him for afternoon tea.

It's ok. He's with Bob and Tess. Bob went up to the hall looking for him. I think he thought the grizzly bear had taken him." She looked sheepishly down to the ground knowing that she had done the wrong thing.

"So is Bob ok?" Mom queried.

"Yes, he's on his way back," Dad replied.

"Should we ask him to sleep in our bus tonight?"

"No, I already did. He's happy to go back to his caravan."

"Has anyone checked the weather report to see what sort of storm we're in for? I'm not so comfortable sleeping under these trees," Mom continued.

"Well, if I was allowed to bring my iPad I could check the radar for you but……." Lisa began, but was interrupted by Dad.

"Yes Bob has. Believe it or not, he has a laptop *and* an iPad in there, and he checked, and it looks like it's going to go around us. Just heavy rains rather than lashing storms."

"Right, well let's find something to eat, now that our other supper was kindly donated to a hungry bear," Mom suggested, looking more at ease.

"Can we go get pizza?" I kindly suggested.

"Der Dork! Like, the nearest pizza place is probably like an hour away and I'm starved," Lisa mumbled.

"Actually Lisa, the nearest pizza place is probably four hours away, and even if it was around the corner, we wouldn't be venturing out for fatty, greasy cheese and dough nutrition, or should I say, lack of nutrition, in this treacherous weather. In fact, even if the weather was perfect, we would be having something that is nutritious. Got it!"

Why doesn't my Mom like take out??? Deprived, we are.

The beds were uncomfortable but I was so exhausted from the excitement of the day, it wasn't long before I drifted off to sleep after our boring supper of salad and bread. The swirling wind kept banging, and the rain poured constantly, but I felt safe knowing that Mom and Dad were just a couple of bus seats away. Occasionally the odd thought of the grizzly bear popped into my head, but the bus was strong and sturdy, even though it was ancient, so I knew it wouldn't be able to get in if it tried.

It wasn't long before I felt myself trekking again in a Minecraft madness dream. This time I was surrounded by a thickly dense forest lined with trees made out of rectangular forms. Everywhere I looked, there were trees. I slashed my way through the forest, finally coming to a raging torrent tunneling

106

through the forest like a snake on a rampage. I was desperate to get to the other side to get to the treasure, but I remembered my dad's words, "Don't go in the river, don't go in the river."

I needed to build a boat or a white water raft to ride the rapids down and get off on the other side. I looked around to see what materials I could muster, and out of the corner of my eye I saw a flash of movement and then an almighty growl curdled through the night air. Expecting to see a Zombie or a creeper, I turned around to see a vicious looking grizzly bear standing on his hind legs, bellowing at me. His eyes were gleaming red and his face enraged as he outstretched his claws into the air. There were only two things on his mind; me and supper.

"Game on Boy," I said to my predator. "You wanna play that game? Well two can play that game," and I reached into my pocket to find a weapon. The game was reversed. I was now the predator and the bear was the prey. I put on my armor and attacked the bear with a sword. The bear then started firing arrows at me, but when they penetrated my armor, the only damage they dealt me was colorful paintball splatters. By the end of the warfare I looked like the Tin Man who had fallen into a rainbow.

Then the whole scenario went totally insane. Instead of the bear falling tragically to his death, he kept stalking me, coming closer and closer, his big hairy arms raised high in the air as he approached my vibrantly colored body. And then the bear did the unthinkable.

23. Don't go Near the River.

Just as I thought my death was near, the bear did an almighty roar that bellowed through the air, then he reached out towards me, and in a surprisingly gentle voice, he spoke. "Huggie," he said, as he grabbed me in the biggest 'bear' hug. I was gob smacked.

My jaw dropped open as I'd never been hugged by a bear before. It was tightening around my neck, blocking off my airways. I struggled to get my breath as the ferocious animal enclosed his arms around me and started shaking me. "Huggie, huggie, huggie," it kept saying. Then the voice started changing, it became more high pitched and the words changed, but the shaking continued. "Wakie, wakie, wakie. Wake up! WAKE UP! WAKE UP!!"

"AGHHHHHHHHHHHH!" I started screaming. It was worse than the bear. It was her again. Why does she always have to wake me up out of a beautiful sleep with her uncontrolled violence all the time? Lisa was shaking me, trying to wake me up. I'd been dreaming about Minecraft again. It was Minecraft madness, but it was better than having your sister lunge at you while you're sleeping. Couldn't she just gently whisper, "Good morning darling favorite brother," or something, instead of this crazed lunatic asylum stuff? Her hair was dripping wet and her bright red face was streaked with smudged black makeup. She looked like a cross between a crazed up Monster High doll and a vampire.

"Something terrible has happened. RYAN! GET UP! Something really bad, you have to go outside and find him."

"What? What are you talking about? Where's Mom and Dad?" I looked around and saw their empty beds. The rain was still falling heavily and the wind had become fierce.

"I found this note on my bed. They've taken Bob to the emergency ward at a hospital two hours away. That's all it says except that we have to take care of the dogs."

I immediately felt a pang of worry, but I knew Bob was in good hands with Mom and Dad, and once he got to the hospital, he'd get the right treatment. He'd be ok.

"Don't worry Lisa. He'll be ok." I sort of put my arm around her and patted her, touched by her concern for the old man.

"No, you don't understand. It's not Bob I'm worried about, well maybe a little bit, but it's the dogs I'm *really* worried about. I woke up because Tess was barking her head off, and she was standing outside our door. She never comes over unless she's allowed. She was trying to tell me something Ryan. I just know it. And I can't find Max. She was trying to tell me that Max is in trouble. And now I can't even find Tess. Come

109

on, you've got to come and help," Lisa frantically rambled. I'd never seen her so upset, except for when she didn't get an iPhone 6 when they first came out.

I looked outside at the drenching rain. "Lisa, it's pouring outside."

"So what?" she said, shaking me by the shoulders. She was right (for a change). It didn't matter if we got saturated or blown around. We had to find the dogs. Apart from the fact that Bob would be devastated if something happened to them, *we* would all be extremely upset as well.

I grabbed my rain jacket, thankful Mom had convinced me to pack it, and stepped into my rain boots. I blasted the door open with brute strength I didn't know I possessed, pushing against the force of the wind. I bounded down the steps and into the rain, and to my horror, I realized I was still in my pajamas; more horrifying was the fact that they were my Thomas ones. I'd had them since I was eight. Not only did they have holes in them, they were definitely too babyish for me.

I glanced around, but the weather had kept most of the campers indoors and it was only early. No one would see me, and even if they did, it was too bad. I didn't have time to care what others thought. The weather looked menacing, as if it might get angrier.

I looked toward Bob's van but the dogs weren't in their basket.

"You don't suppose Bob might have put Maxi inside last night?"

"No, I had a little peek. He's definitely not there. HURRY Ryan." I looked over towards the river which had become a raging torrent overnight. The small trickling waterfalls had turned into angry rapids cascading forcefully over the rocks. They looked frightening and I thought about Dad's wise words, "don't go near the river." He was a wise man that's for sure.

In the distance I could hear the strangled sounds of a dog barking somewhere. Lisa and I looked at each other. "Tess," we both said simultaneously. I started to run through the forest in the direction of the sound, until finally, I saw Tess standing on the edge of the river bank yelping fretfully.

"Is she ok?" Lisa said, as she caught up to me when I approached the dog.

"It's ok girl, it's ok. You're ok now," I said to the dog as she jumped up and down licking me. I looked her over but she didn't seem to be injured, just stressed. She circled on the spot and then turned away from me, back to the river and started barking again. I scanned the area but it was hard to see further than ten meters because of the rain pelting down.

"THERE!" Lisa screamed in a high pitched voice, blowing my eardrum into smithereens. She pointed wildly at something out in the middle of the river.

"OH NO!" My heart sank, and the thumping gremlin that lived inside me suddenly grew to infestation levels, and the pounding inside my throat raged like the torrent that lay in front of me.

24. Too Young to Die

I wiped the rain from my face and rubbed my eyes to get a better visual. Both Lisa and I looked at each other not knowing what we could do to help. She looked as bedraggled as I felt in her sodden dressing gown and her drenched hair. My rain coat was keeping my body dry but my head was copping the pelting rain, stinging my cheeks.

"Ryan you have to do something," Lisa begged.

"What? What can I do? You know Dad said we're not allowed in the river, and that was when it was calm. Go and get a grown up to help. I'll wait here and keep watch."

"No one is around. It will be too late. Maxi will fall in." I looked over to the trembling dog stranded in the middle of the waterway clinging to a rock. Tess was barking constantly towards the little animal and she returned a frightened gaze back to her friend. The last thing I wanted was for Tess to try and jump in and save her mate, but I could see she was thinking about it, as she kept edging closer to the water nervously.

"Lisa hold Tess back. I'm afraid she might slip, then we'll have to save the both of them."

I looked around again, hoping there was an adult around. We were too far into the forest, and the wind and rain were so loud, nobody would have been able to hear the commotion for miles.

I kept hearing Dad's voice in my head, "don't go in the river," like over and over again. I wasn't only petrified of getting into trouble, I was absolutely horrified at the thought of getting dragged under the water by one of those Eddy Kruger things Dad had been talking about. I was a strong swimmer, but the thought of drowning in a raging torrent really didn't thrill me at all. It had always been a dream of mine to go white water rafting, but not without a raft! And definitely not without a life jacket.

"Lisa, Dad's gonna be stinkin' mad if I go in there."

"Who cares? Just tell him I forced you."

"Really? You'd say that?"

"YES! Anything to save Maxi. Oh forget it. I'll do it." She ripped off her dressing gown and started taking off her slippers. I thought she might have been bluffing until she started wading out, the cold water taking her breath away.

"Lisa get out of there. You're not a strong swimmer."

"Well I don't have much choice do I?" As we argued on the bank, Tess's barks got louder, and a gush of water pushed Max into the river.

"OHHHH," Lisa shrieked, becoming hysterical as the tiny dog scrambled onto the rock before slipping again. His little feet worked overtime as he managed to get back to a safer position higher on the rock. I knew it would only be a matter of time before another gush would throw him off again, so I tossed my rain jacket off and kicked my boots aside and waded out as far as I could stand. The water left me breathless with each icy blow shocking my body.

I had no idea what I was doing. I knew it was wrong, but every part of me could not stand there and watch a helpless dog drown. I had visions of the newspaper headlines the next day, 'Boy Drowns Saving Dog' or 'Boy becomes hero saving dog but he doesn't know because he drowned'.

I wanted to turn back. I didn't want to die. I was too young. I still had so many things I wanted to do in my life. I still had so many buildings left to build on Minecraft and I hadn't had a chance to save up and buy Destiny yet, *and* I still wasn't old enough to get Halo either. Hek, I hadn't even kissed a girl. Ok that wouldn't worry me if I didn't get round to that.

Tess had stopped barking because she knew the rescue team were onto it, and I could see Max's tail wagging, though he was still shivering uncontrollably. I struggled to keep my footing as the river bottom fell away. I lunged into the waters, and propelled myself against the current, exhausted from the rapids scurrying around me.

The wind howled in the trees above and thunder started to roll in the distance, and the rain kept thrashing. I felt like I was right in the middle of a movie set on the film 'Rescue of Lassie the dog', but when I looked around, there were no movie cameras, booms, green screens, or director's chairs and, unfortunately, no adults. Just Tess and Lisa and her iPhone. WHAT!?.....LISA WAS VIDEOING ON HER iPHONE!

"Are you crazy? Stop filming. Go and get help or something. Lisa stop filming!" Water gushed in my mouth as I yelled, surging into openings where it wasn't welcome, causing me to splutter and gasp again. I couldn't believe she would have the stupidity to video the event. What was she doing? Did she want evidence to get me into trouble? Surely she couldn't be that spiteful. I couldn't think about it. I had to concentrate on getting to Maxi and saving his life (and mine as well).

Then all thoughts abandoned my mind as the river enveloped me and sucked me away from my intended path, dragging me under. I felt something brush past my leg, and prayed that it was just a weed or a twig.

115

I gasped for breath as I propelled myself to the surface, just in time to reach out and grab a spindly branch from a broken tree. 'Thank you Mom for forcing me to go to all those swimming lessons and squad training,' I thought to myself, 'even though I cried when it was Winter'.

I held onto the branch tightly, trying to catch my breath, letting the freezing water run rapidly over my body and sheltering my mouth so it didn't trespass again.

"Go Ryan! Go Ryan!" I could hear in the distance. I didn't have the energy to look back or call out to shut her up. I just had to soldier on, and just as I made the decision to let go of the branch, it cut loose from its anchor and hurtled off down the river. I lunged further with my arms into the water, my limbs numb from the cold, not feeling anything. I became one with the water. The water and I together were on a mission to save the poor animal.

I was within two meters of reaching out to Maxi when an almighty crack boomed from high above, mingled with the sounds of Lisa screeching hysterically. In the split second I had to think about it, I didn't know whether I was being shot at, about to be struck by lightning or some other evil force of nature.

I looked up to see a gigantic branch tumbling from its perch, falling in my direction. There was nothing I could do to prevent an unfortunate tragedy, but to dive into the murky waters, and hope the branch would be carried downstream on impact. My life was in the hands of the Gods.

25. Out of my Depth

A world of darkness enveloped me as I sunk into the depths of the river, holding my breath for as long as I could. All those times Mom used to tell me off for holding my breath underwater came in handy as I blocked my airways and held on tightly.

I could hear the forceful sound of the branch smashing into the water, creating a gurgling vacuum as it ploughed to the bottom, but nothing appeared to slash me, so I once again propelled myself out of the water and into the daylight, and prayed harder that Maxi would be ok. When I opened my eyes, my heart drowned in sadness as I desperately looked for a little dog that wasn't there anymore.

26. Courage and Determination

Adrenaline powered through my body, and a new found strength rose up through every atom I had, as I dolphined through the water looking for him.

"THERE!" Lisa screamed. "He's over there."

I could hear her calling but I couldn't see where she was. I was totally disorientated floundering in a bubbling and gushing body of water. My head felt dizzy and my arms started to feel like lumps of lead dragging them through the water.

I remembered Miss Dorkland's words, 'Just have courage and determination, and a little bit of encouragement from your friends will help'. I definitely had encouragement from Lisa, and I was determined enough to find Maxi, but I was worried I didn't have the courage to keep going through the treacherous conditions.

Lisa's voice was becoming more high pitched and hysterical. It was a wonder the whole camping ground couldn't hear her. It was the one time in my life I wanted her to shriek so loud that she annoyed everyone close by, but it was the only time that she didn't.

"Maxi!" I shrieked, when I saw a little white head tumbling away from me with two little legs paddling furiously. His little face was full of anguish, but he was too far away now, and travelling too fast for me to reach out.

'Have courage Rino. Have courage and determination', I heard the voices in my head say.

BUTTERFLY! I hate butterfly stroke. But with three full strokes I could be close to Max if I pounced straight away, and I would be able to see where I was going at the same time.

Courage: *You **can** do it.*

Determination: *I **will** do it*

I leapt into the air,

ONCE. *There he is.*

TWICE. *Come on buddy, stay where you are*

THREE TIMES. *Ok, still need one more*

FOURTH: *Gottcha!!! Maxi, gottcha.*

Now what?

Courage & Determination

27. Blackness

Now for Life saving side stroke.

I learnt that in surf lifesaving skills in squad training. Dog under left arm and stroke with right arm and hope the victim doesn't panic and drown you. This would be the first time I'd done it with a dog though. The rest were either with other kids or practice dummies. The dog was definitely a lot lighter.

Head for the bank.

Courage and determination. You can do it! You can do it!

Head for the bank. The bank, the bank, the bank, the bank............. the bank..................... the....

BLACKNESS!

28. Drowning

"Is he ok? Call 911. HELP! Somebody get some help."

Faces, all over the place, screaming, shouting. *Was I in trouble? I was in trouble. I swam in the river. Why did I swim in the river? Now I was in trouble.*

"I'm sorry Mom, sorry. I had to do it." *Why did I have to do it?*

"It's ok boy. Stay calm. You got no need to be sorry boy. You're a hero. You saved the puppy."

BLACKNESS AGAIN

"Ryan wake up! Please wake up."

The shaking, the uncontrollable shaking. There it was again, always shaking me when I wanted to sleep. I opened my eyes gingerly. They were burning and itchy and the right one seemed to be covered with something, but I managed to make out the figure looming down on me. It was her again.

"Lisa?" I said breathlessly. "Am I in trouble?"

"No you big dope. You're a hero. You're my hero. Everything's going to be ok. You saved Maxi. The ambulance is on the way."

"I saved Max? What's wrong with him and why does he need an ambulance?"

"Just rest son," a strange voice said from above me. "Your parents are going to be here soon." Suddenly I felt an intense pain across the right side of my face and my right shoulder, throbbing and burning, and I couldn't see out of my right eye. Something seemed to be covering it.

I looked out of my left eye and realized I was lying on the blow up bed in our annex. I had no idea how I got there or for how long I'd been sleeping. There were several people surrounding me, but I couldn't recognize them except for Lisa. All I know is, they were being very nice and very caring towards me for some reason, and the pain was KILLING ME!

As the sounds of an ambulance siren echoed in the distance, snippets of the past couple of hours came filtering through my mind like a jigsaw puzzle, but I couldn't put the pieces together. It was like the jigsaw had been scattered across the floor, only it was me across the floor.

I put my hand up to rub my eye but touched something wet and soggy. As I brought it down again, I winced when I saw it was covered in blood. Where had the blood come from? Had Max been injured?

My mind kept racing, fighting off flashes of the past; roaring thunder, flashes of light, trees crashing, bears, sirens, and water; lots of water everywhere. I felt like I was drowning; drowning in my own thoughts of water. My mind was filling with water, my lungs were filling with water.

Drowning.

I just wanted to sleep. I wanted to block the pain. The pain was intense, in my face and my legs and everywhere.

"Don't go to sleep son. Stay awake," a lady rubbed my shoulders as she spoke to me. And why was everyone calling me son? I wasn't their son. I was Mom and Dad's son. But they weren't with me.

I tried to gain clarity and understand the situation, but my mind wasn't playing the game. I wanted to sleep and fall into one of my Minecraft madness dreams. But these strangers weren't playing the game. They weren't letting me sleep. Couldn't they see I hadn't had any sleep?

I............NEEDED.............. SLEEP!

29. Minecraft Jokes and Cool Bananas

The ambulance ride to the hospital was a blurry haze. All I could remember was seeing Mom's worried face looking down on me, as I was sucking on this awesome green lollypop whistle thing. I'd never had one of those lollypops before. I wondered where we could get some more. They made me feel like……

Weeeeeeeee

Squeeeeeeeeeeeeeeeeee

Cool bananas

Cool baby

How are you doin'?

Mom told me later that I kept cracking all these silly jokes about Minecraft like, "why are zombies afraid of me? Because I get them all fired up." And, "why don't I like deep, dark caves in Minecraft? Because they drive me batty." OH dear. My humor wasn't too good when I was in lala land.

She also told me that the green lollypop had pain relief medication in it that makes you go a bit loopy, because I was apparently screaming and in a lot of pain when the ambulance men had arrived. In the emergency ward, I was given eighteen stitches for a 10 cm gash that went across my face, just nicking the corner of my eye, which is why I had to wear a patch for the next week. I also had to have stitches in both my legs and I had deep cuts all over my body that they had to glue up.

Apparently I'd been slashed by a falling tree and I hadn't even felt it. Lisa said she had it all on her iPhone. Mom and Dad were a bit cross with her because we weren't supposed to take electronics on our trip, but I think they were sort of pleased she videoed it, because we got to relive the experience, like again and again and again. She was warned very severely about not putting it on Face Book though, despite the fact she's not allowed to have a Face Book account anyway. I think Mom turns a blind eye to the fact that she does. Ouch, don't talk about blind eyes, it hurts.

She wanted to take a photo of me and put it on back chat or instra thingie, or whatever you call it, but I wouldn't let her. There was no way I was having my mug the way it looked, out there for all the world to laugh at. Dad said I looked like Jack Sparrow out of 'Pirates of the Carribean'.

Before we left the hospital, we got to visit Bob. I was allowed to leave after I had scans and they sewed me up with a needle and cotton, but poor old Bob had to stay in for a few days. Apparently he'd had a mild heart attack, and if Mom and Dad hadn't acted so quickly and got him to the hospital, things might have been a lot worse. My parents were awesome!

And I guess Lisa was pretty awesome sometimes too. When Mom and Dad arrived at the same time as the ambos, they said she was holding my head in her arms and stroking it. When I heard that, I really didn't know whether to puke or cry. She was also the one who apparently dragged me up the bank and ran to get help carrying the dog to safety at the same time. So I guess I should be grateful that she didn't just leave me there to die, (though I'm sure she was tempted).

Dad drove us back to the camping ground in Bob's car. While I rested, Mum and Dad helped the Park manager to pack up Bob's stuff. The weather had eased considerably and sunlight was starting to sprinkle its charm throughout the trees.

When I woke several hours later, a very tired Max was lying on my chest and Tess was on the ground, at my feet, snoring. Lisa was reading peacefully on her bed, not bugging me for a change. For a moment I thought I'd died and gone to heaven.

In the morning, the pain was intense in my eye, but it was nothing compared to the intensity of the pain I felt in my heart, because I knew we were about to go home. I had no idea when, or if, I would ever see my little mates again. Solemnly, I got myself ready, cleaning my teeth without eating breakfast, trying to push back rebel tears that threatened to start falling like waterfalls. And I'd had enough waterfalls for the weekend.

Our annex had been pulled down so the dogs sat in the warm sunshine next to our bus. Dad had brought over their basket the night before, but they stayed most of the night next to me, panting and dribbling gooey stuff all over the place. Lisa was acting really weird all morning, and being so nice to me. It was totally out of character for her. Maybe Mom had told her to be nice to me. I'm sure she wouldn't have come up with that idea on her own.

At 10 o'clock, Dad ordered us onto the bus, like a train conductor. "All aboard. Last bus headed for the homelands. Toot Toot."

"What about the dogs Dad? We have to put them safely away over at Bob's caravan," I said, gently stroking the dogs with each hand, one on each side of me, "so we don't run over them."

"Ah they'll get out of the way. They're not silly."

My heart crumbled at Dad's coldness. How could he just think that the dogs would just wander back to their caravan? Both of them were looking up at me with mournful eyes, wanting me to rescue them.

"If I could, I would put you both in my bags," I whispered to them, "but my life wouldn't be worth living if I smuggled you home. It's ok, Bob will take good care of you." And as I spoke those words to the dogs, I had the most terrible realization.

Bob wasn't coming back anytime soon!

"DAAAAAAD!!"

30. Heartbreak Time.

Dad flicked the switch and pumped the gas, and the old machine snarled into action. Mom was sitting in the front seat reading a boring women's magazine, probably about celebrities and divorces, babies and yukky recipes. Lisa was sitting in her seat with her iPhone behind a book, pretending to read. No-one seemed to care about the poor little dogs left without their owner for 'who knew how long'.

"Dad, we forgot, Bob's not coming home! The dogs will be by themselves," I said still panicking.

"They'll be right mate. They'll fend for themselves. Tess will go and get them a wild animal for their supper, and they can shelter from the weather under that tree next to Bob's caravan."

I looked from my Dad to the helpless animals staring up at me as I stood on the step. How could he be so cold and emotionless? I was more shocked with Lisa that she wasn't making a scene about taking Max. Surely she would have tried to smuggle him into her bag? But he was just moping around, next to Tess, knowing something terrible was about to happen.

"Dad." My voice cracked as I tried to hold back the tears, failing dismally. "We can't just leave them to fend for themselves."

"You're right son. I'll get the park manager to go up and feed them tonight."

"Will we ever see them again?"

"Who knows mate? Bob doesn't live all that close, but maybe back here one day. Come on bud, get on the bus. The sooner we get going, the sooner you can go home and have a game of PlayStation."

PlayStation? Who wanted to play PlayStation, or XBOX or Minecraft or anything when these little things would be left all alone? I gave them the biggest hug and nuzzled my head into their warm bodies letting my tears run off their fur. Slowly I walked up the steps as if I was walking the plank to my death on a pirate ship, although I was the one that looked like the pirate.

"Ah mate, can you pass me my jacket before we start? It's in that cupboard." Dad pointed to one of the cupboards in the bus.

I opened the cupboard and looked for Dad's jacket. I couldn't see it, but a tin can rolled out and hit me on the toe. Just what I needed.

"It's not here Dad. Just tins of….." I looked closer to see what they were. "Just tins of dog food. DOG FOOD? WHY IS THERE DOG FOOD IN OUR BUS?"

They were all staring at me, laughing.

"Come on boy, come on Tess, Dad said to the dogs. "Let's go. Oh I almost forgot to tell you. Bob only has a sister who lives in a flat so Mom offered to look after the dogs until he gets out of hospital."

"SERIOUSLY?" I could feel my eyes lighting up like a Christmas tree. "AW MAN! You had me going there. I seriously thought you were cruel as."

"Cruel as what?"

"Just cruel as. Wow I'm so glad your heart isn't made of stone."

Awesome. It was just, insanely awesome. I felt like all my Christmases had come at once. I didn't care if I never had another Christmas present in my life. I didn't care if I never played the PlayStation 4 again. I didn't care if I never played Minecraft again. Well maybe I *was* getting a bit carried away with all the promises.

129

31. My Awesome Family

Mom wouldn't let me go to school for a couple of days, which was torture because I really wanted to tell Matthew and Josh about the weekend and the dogs and everything. I also wanted to thank Miss Dorklands for her words of encouragement that helped me save Maxi.

Matthew ran up to me as soon as he saw me before the bell rang.

"What the? Who are you, Pirate Pete?" I had to wear my patch to school so I was ready for the teasing and the name calling. Kids can't help themselves, even your so-called friends have to have a bit of a stir.

"Yeah I had a little bit of a run in with a tree," I said modestly.

"How was the camping? Boring I bet?" Matthew asked. "My Mom told me you were going. I felt really sorry for you. And I thought you were going to miss out on my party."

I laughed. "You *thought* I was going to miss your party. News

flash! I *did* miss your party."

"News flash for you. You *didn't* miss my party. I cancelled it."

"For real? Why? Did you get into trouble?"

"Nah. Don't be stupid. I never get into trouble," he grinned. "There was too much cyclonic rain, and it was unsafe to drive Mom said. And a couple of people had already cancelled because of the stinkin' weather anyway."

"Ah too bad." I felt really sorry for Matthew, but I started to secretly get a little excited.

"Nah it's all good. Now I can get my best buddy to come when we have it next week."

"For real?"

"For real!"

"Awesome." Last week I had been doing double back flips, triple whammy somersaults followed by a forward pike at the thought of Matthew's party. But now, it was kinda like, oh yeah, that's cool. Man, how I had changed in one weekend.

"So how was it then? Was there fun stuff? Were there any adventure parks? Any adrenaline junky activities?"

"Oh yeah, there was definitely fun stuff and definitely adventure, and definitely activities to get my adrenaline going."

"So did you get much rain on your camping trip?"

"Ah yeah! You could say that. It rained cats and dogs all weekend! Mainly dogs. And now it's still raining dogs even though the sun is shining," I said, laughing to myself.

He looked at me weirdly and I smiled back at him. Yet another example of my Mom's old philosophy, '*sometimes good things can come out of bad*'.

Yep!

The End.

Don't forget, if you liked this book, please tell your friends and leave a review on Amazon or Goodreads.

You may also like other books by this author

available from Amazon as ebooks or print books

Game on Boys 1: The PlayStation Playoffs

Game on Boys 3 : No Girls allowed

Game on Boys 4 : Minecraft Superhero

Diary Of a Wickedly Cool Witch : Bullies and Baddies

Made in the USA
Monee, IL
13 February 2022

91226782R00075